Every Teacher's
Guide to
Working With
PARENTS

Every Teacher's
Guide to
Working With
PARENTS

GWEN L. RUDNEY

CORWIN PRESS
A SAGE Publications Company
Thousand Oaks, California

For information:

Corwin Press
A Sage Publications Company
2455 Teller Road
Thousand Oaks, California 91320
www.corwinpress.com

Sage Publications Ltd.
1 Oliver's Yard
55 City Road
London EC1Y 1SP
United Kingdom

Sage Publications India Pvt. Ltd.
B-42, Panchsheel Enclave
Post Box 4109
New Delhi 110 017 India

Printed in the United States of America.

Library of Congress Cataloging-in-Publication Data

Rudney, Gwen L.
Every teacher's guide to working with parents / Gwen L. Rudney.
    p. cm.
Includes bibliographical references and index.
ISBN 1-4129-1774-3 (cloth)—ISBN 1-4129-1775-1 (pbk.)
    1. Parent-teacher relationships—Handbooks, manuals, etc. I. Title.
LC226.R83 2005
371.103—dc22   2005008040

This book is printed on acid-free paper.

05   06   07   08   09   10   9   8   7   6   5   4   3   2   1

Acquisitions Editor:	Faye Zucker
Editorial Assistant:	Gem Rabanera
Production Editor:	Laureen A. Shea
Copy Editor:	Stacey Shimizu
Typesetter:	C&M Digitals (P) Ltd.
Proofreader:	Sally M. Scott
Indexer:	Nara Wood
Cover Designer:	Michael Dubowe
Graphic Designer:	Scott Van Atta

Contents

Preface

My daughter has always been a worrier, but my husband and I appreciate her reflective qualities. She is a deep thinker and acts in thoughtful ways. As I was tucking her into bed one night when she was about eight, I could tell she was upset. She looked at me with her serious, round, blue eyes and said, "Why is the news always so bad?" She had heard somehow about a father who had put his child in an oil drum while he went to work. I told her that the news is often bad because the bad stuff is more rare than the good. That's what makes it news. There isn't enough time to report the name of every parent who gave his or her child a goodnight kiss before tucking the child in or who put the child in a car seat and drove carefully to a safe, licensed, and caring day care before going to work. Those activities happen over and over, day after day, in neighborhood after neighborhood. I told her that the father had done a very bad thing, and that people were going to help the little boy and his dad. Most parents take care of their kids. It's just not news when they do so.

Maybe it should be the news. The message that most parents are good enough is one of the reasons that I wanted to write this book for teachers and others who care about positive parent-teacher relationships. When parents and teachers work together, great things can happen. This book will provide an accurate and useful interpretation of parent beliefs and actions. In Chapter 1, you will learn new information, concepts, and viewpoints that you can use in personal and professional interactions with—or about—parents. The chapter is designed to help you review, expand, and consolidate your existing knowledge base about parents and parenting. The information in Chapter 2 provides insight into what parents expect from teachers. It offers practical suggestions that individual teachers can use to improve communication and collaboration with parents. Chapter 3 explores key ideas that characterize some of the troubles and troublesome attitudes that parents face as they work to raise children in today's society. This final chapter has an advocacy focus for children *and* their families.

Speaking of families, I would like you to meet mine so that you know a little about me before reading my words. I grew up in southern California, where I attended (and later taught in) schools rich in diversity. I was an only child, and both my parents worked. I am Lutheran, but my parents did not attend church while I was growing up. I made the decision to attend church on my own when I was in my early 20s. I taught sixth and seventh grade language arts and social studies for 13 years before beginning my work in the university setting. I have been married to Steve for 22 years. He is of Russian Jewish heritage, but was not raised in the Jewish tradition. It is a second marriage for both of us. My son Paul was four when Steve and I were married. My ex-husband stopped seeing Paul regularly after that, but Paul stayed in contact with his paternal grandparents. Paul calls Steve "Dad," and Steve considers Paul his son. Steve and his ex-wife did not have children.

When Paul was a sophomore in college, he showed up at home by surprise one day. He said that he needed to talk to us upstairs. That meant he needed privacy and that it was important. He told us that he was gay. I gave him a big hug and said, "This isn't going to affect your schooling, is it?" and he laughed out loud. He said, "That's what I told everybody you would say!" As it turned out it, he did drop out after coming out . . . but he has gathered remarkable experiences and continues to pursue his dreams.

Our daughter Cara is in her second year of college and is planning to be—much to her own surprise—a teacher. We are thrilled for her and her future students. She is musical and sweet. She is an honors student, and we find it funny that she is the only one of our children to be sent to the principal's office for misbehaving during an assembly.

Phil is our youngest and is still in high school. He is a good student and a lot of fun to have around. He didn't much like being the youngest when he was little. He started to cry when Cara came home from school in first grade and read a book to him. He said, "Now I'm the only one in this family who can't read." He was three and a half! Phil is musical and athletic. He is the only one in the family who actually *likes* to work out. We have learned a lot about basketball because of him.

My family is a blended family with different perspectives and experiences. Well positioned in the middle class, we enjoy many advantages. Yet there are aspects of our lives and experiences that have brought us both shared and unique challenges. Every family has a story.

Though the concepts and suggestions you will read are situated in a largely *professional* setting, they are indeed *personal.* You will find the focus here on what *one* person—each of us— can do to improve relationships with others. I hope that the perspectives and strategies you will read help you to build positive relationships that are honest and respectful and that ultimately improve life, success, joy, growth, and learning for children.

Acknowledgments

I am indebted to my colleagues and friends at the University of Minnesota, Morris, for their help and encouragement through this astonishing process. The faculty and staff in the Division of Education are wonderful models of excellence and my inspiration. I appreciate the feedback and the fun they provide. I am grateful for the conscientious and invaluable work completed by my Morris Academic Partner, Bettina Mohn.

I also want to acknowledge the interest and enthusiasm shown by my students throughout this process. I would like to name every one of them here, but, instead, I want them to know that they are forever in my heart.

—Gwen L. Rudney

Corwin Press thanks the following reviewers for their contributions to this work:

Vickie Catalina, Teacher
Stephens Elementary/Middle School
Detroit, MI

Monica Swartz Haeussler, Gifted Program Instructor
Barclay and Titus Elementary Schools
Warringtown, PA

Jodie Heliker, Reading Resource Specialist
Kottmeyer School
St. Louis, MO

Kathryn McCormick, Teacher
Gahanna Middle School East
Gahanna, OH

Cami Sullivan, Gifted Language Arts Teacher
Smokey Road Middle School
Newnan, GA

Tony Vincent, Teacher
Millard Public Schools
Omaha, NE

Karen Walker, Speech Language Pathologist
Harold Schnell Elementary School
West Carrollton, OH

About the Author

Gwen L. Rudney, PhD, is an Associate Professor of Education at the University of Minnesota, Morris. She is an active member of the American Educational Research Association and the National Association for Multicultural Education. She was a teacher of language arts and social studies at the middle school level for 13 years. Her teaching and research interests now include classroom processes, teacher development, multicultural education, and working with parents. Dr. Rudney has worked with student teachers and cooperating teachers in regional, national, and international settings. She is coauthor of *Maximum Mentoring: An Action Guide for Teacher Trainers and Cooperating Teachers.* She enjoys serving as the chair of the Minnesota Teacher of the Year Program. In 2004, she received the University of Minnesota, Morris, Alumni Teaching Award.

With love and gratitude, I dedicate this book to my family:

*To my husband, Steve Rudney, and my children,
Paul Halacy, Cara Rudney, and Philip Rudney*

*To my parents, Milton and Adair Horgen, and in memory of my
grandparents, Everett and Mily Phelps and Albert and Gina Horgen*

*With encouragement and appreciation,
I also dedicate this book to the teachers and parents who
work tirelessly together to make the world a better place for every child.*

1

Understanding the Lives of Parents

Why Do They Do Those Things They Do?

Scenario: "If the Parents Would Just . . ."

The teacher workroom was buzzing with early-morning preparation for the day's classes. Janice, an eighth grade science teacher, shared her frustration about her class with a colleague. "I have worked so hard this year to increase the hands-on lab experiments with my students. To have it work, though, they need to have done the reading. Every day, the same kids come in without their homework done. I have called home and sent messages, but nothing seems to happen. If the parents would just . . ."

"If the parents would just . . . , then there would be no problem." I have often heard this phrase when listening to teachers—even good ones—complain about a child or teenager doing something wrong or not doing something right. Lots of people say it. I have said it too. But I don't say it anymore. I have learned that taking the fast track to blaming parents rarely captures the whole truth of a situation and almost never is helpful. If teachers and others who care about children—and that means most of us—are truly interested in providing the best kind of world for young people, then they—we—need to appreciate the complexity of parenthood and the demands made of those who parent.

Adults who work with children and families can improve interactions, collaboration, and necessary interventions, if they first understand and respect the nature, dynamics, and complexities of parenting. The purpose of this chapter is to help build that understanding. In this chapter, we examine what parenting entails and what "good parenting" *may* look like. We explore the messages that parents receive and some of the demands that they must meet. All of this information adds to the teacher's knowledge base for success in building relationships.

DEMANDS AND DECISIONS

Parenthood is hard. In my work with teachers, my first and foremost goal is to help them see and understand the difficulties of parenting—even for relatively happy, healthy, and "normal" parents. Parenting involves responding to a constant stream of demands and making decision after decision. Parents may not even be aware of the constancy of the decision-making process. But they most certainly feel the demands. Take, for example, the times when children "loosen their belts." That is what I call what happens when parents pick up their children at day care or greet them as they come home from school. Most children—even teenagers—save up their concerns for the people with whom they feel safest and the place where they feel they can "let it out." Galinsky (2001) calls it the "arsenic hour," and the demands made of parents are high. Parents must decide how to accept their children's right to be comfortable and safe at home, and at the same time maintain and model self-respect and a healthy environment. Cassidy (1998) reminds parents that they can't let their children walk all over them just because they feel safe. There are always competing needs and goals, demands and decisions.

If we were to list the dimensions and demands of parenting, how long would the list be? What would we include? Parents certainly need to feed, clothe, and shelter their children. What is the best way? They need to encourage both independence and kindness toward others. How do they do so? They need to praise and give constructive criticism. When and where? The goal of parents, even in different times and different places, is to protect and prepare their children (Fuller & Olsen, 2003). How they go about meeting that important goal differs from parent to parent, and some attempts are more successful than others.

Most parents worry, for example, about how best to discipline their children. They consider rules, consequences, beliefs about physical punishment, verbal responses, work expectations, behavior in public, behavior at home, and scores of other things. Any parenting element would also have subcategories. What does this mean for parents? Mostly it means that, whether or not they think about it all the time (and they can't), they are managing and functioning within a complex context.

In addition to the type of decisions, we have to understand the *number* of decisions that parents must make. Every day there are hundreds. Some are little. Anna didn't put away her crayons. Some are big. Tonya said she was going to Marie's house, but she went to the movies with Isaiah instead. And some are frighteningly huge. Maria is talking about suicide. Yes, parents make hundreds of decisions every day. Most of them are based on their children's well being, and some are geared to the safeguarding of the children's very souls.

WHAT EXPERTS HAVE TO SAY

Parents have a seemingly unlimited supply of advice, suggestions, tips, and how-to information available from a variety of sources. Different parents will at different times solicit information from experts, and they also will receive unsolicited information from sources and agencies. In this section, we examine samples of this information to see the picture of good parenting they paint. Finally, we explore a theoretical look at parenting styles. In each case, we usually see that parenting well is easier said than done.

Quick Tips on Important Issues

Brochures, pamphlets, and flyers provide critical and concise information about how parents can work with their children through normal stages or special problems. Available from schools, churches, community organizations, and both state and national agencies, the brochures are often mailed to the homes or displayed on tables at various school functions. They often include reasonable advice.

One sample pamphlet is *Another Ten Tips for Parents to Help Their Children Avoid Teen Pregnancy* (National Campaign to Prevent Teen Pregnancy, 1998). The organization encourages parents to be clear in their own attitudes and to talk with their children about sex. Parents should supervise their children's behavior, including what they watch, read, and listen to. They should know about their children's friends and families. When guiding their children through adolescence, parents should discourage early steady dating and dating someone much older or younger. Parents should share their valuing of education and help their children see future opportunities. These clear statements are unarguably good ideas. They are important and project an image of parents who know what they believe, know how to communicate articulately and sensitively with their children, and apparently exercise a reasonable amount of control and influence over their children.

In the tenth tip, the authors recognize the "largeness" of the task. They say,

These first nine tips for helping your children avoid teen pregnancy work best when they occur as part of strong, close relationships with your children that are built from an early age. Strive for a relationship that is warm in tone, firm in discipline, and rich in communication, and one that emphasizes mutual trust and respect. There is no single way to create such relationships, but the following habits of the heart can help. (p. 4)

The helpful habits include expressing love and affection, paying attention, and listening carefully. Parents should spend time with their children and should be supportive and interested in what interests them. And parents should be courteous and respectful toward their children.

Other brochures follow similar patterns of presentation. They are easy to read, typically contain accurate information, and are readily available. They also suffer from a high concept load in that the many quick suggestions included usually entail a great deal more knowledge and skill than provided in the materials.

Popular Literature

Many parents actively seek the advice of experts. Visiting the parenting section of any bookstore or entering *parents* as a search term for online shopping will yield hundreds of selections for interested readers. Some good ones by physicians or child development experts focus on the specific needs of children at different stages and seem to provide good answers for questions that some parents have. A generation ago, many parents were reading Dr. Spock. Currently, the work of Brazelton (Brazelton & Sparrow, 2003) and Leach (Shore, Leach, Sears, Sears, & Weininger, 2002) are especially popular.

Other books focus less on the children and more on parenting behaviors. Author Donna Corwin (1997), for example, offers five categories of parenting. *The fixer*, *the controller*, and *the avoider* are styles that are self-explanatory. Style four is *the modernist* who focuses on psychology and therapy. The fifth style is *the old guard*, who is a throwback to previous generations and may not understand the experiences and expectations of modern children. Corwin states that the styles aren't meant to label, but rather to help understand "parenting traps." The traps she defines are the habits, behaviors, and attitudes that can interfere with effective parenting. Examples include parental attitudes towards sports, beauty, and academics. For each trap, she offers do's and don'ts, which—though not wrong or bad—are simplistic and certainly belie the difficulty of parental success in all areas. They are, of course, easier said than done. Corwin, like others, believes that problems can be rooted in parents' own upbringing and goes on to suggest confronting one's own parents in order to repair and reattach.

That is only *one* book. Others offer advice for helping children as they begin elementary school. Still others guide and comfort parents as they send their children off to college. The experts instruct parents on how to raise successful daughters and caring sons. Parents can read about steps or programs or coping skills to lead them through an array of ordinary and extraordinary parenting situations. I tend to support the ideas of much of the literature—as long as the ideas are considered tools in the parenting toolbox. I am reluctant to say, "This is it. Here's the one. This is what will work for me, for my family, and forever!"

A Theoretical Look at Parenting Styles

Parents strive to protect and prepare their children for life in the world. Of course, how that goal is approached and achieved varies greatly. Diana Baumrind (as cited in Darling, 1999) established categories of parenting that many child development experts analyze and report (see also Harris, 1998; Moore, 1992; Robertson, 1997). She developed the categories by looking at parents' child-rearing behaviors and interactions on two dimensions: nurturance and control. Highly nurturing parents tended to be very child centered and responsive to the special needs of their children, whereas low-nurturance parents tended to focus more on their own expectations for their children's behavior. Parents who were very controlling tended to be quite demanding and quick to confront their children if disobedient, and parents less concerned with control were, as one would expect, less likely to make demands, establish rules, or use confrontational approaches to problems.

Baumrind described three main parenting styles: authoritative, permissive, and authoritarian. According to Harris (1998), these three styles can be characterized as "too hard, too soft, and just right" (p. 47). The "too hard" authoritarian parents are strict. They provide structured environments, enforce clear and rigid rules, and are less responsive to the changing demands of their children. Always directive in dealing with their children, they may also (but not necessarily) be intrusive and autocratic. The children of these parents tend to perform moderately well in school. Though they reportedly exhibit few problem behaviors, they have also shown poorer social skills.

Permissive parents are "too soft" in that they are child centered but undemanding. They can be unclear and inconsistent in establishing structure or expectations. The children of permissive parents tend not to fare as well academically and behaviorally in school. Interestingly, they show better social skills and lower levels of depression.

Authoritative parents are those some consider to be "just right." They can be distinctly supportive while expecting their children to behave. In their attention to the children, they provide clear and careful explanations so that the children can understand expectations. The children of authoritative parents tend to exhibit high levels of academic achievement and social competence and have fewer behavioral problems (Darling, 1999).

Categorizing parents on the two dimensions of nurturance and control, as shown in Table 1.1, actually creates four parenting styles. A fourth style, in which the parents exhibit both low nurturance and low control, is called *uninvolved* (Maccoby & Martin, as cited in Darling, 1999). Uninvolved parenting, with few demands and little responsiveness, results in detachment and lack of commitment to the children. The children of these parents demonstrate the lowest levels of performance in all areas.

The parenting style research, then, suggests that the best parenting involves setting reasonable limits in a child-centered and nurturing environment. When carried out, this style results in increased levels of confidence and achievement for children.

Table 1.1   Styles of Parenting

	Moderate to High Control	*Low Control*
High Nurturance	Authoritative (Moderate Control) • Respond with affection and consideration to child's needs • Provide support and encouragement • Set, explain, and provide rationale for behavioral standards • Avoid extremes	Permissive • May be nontraditional • Allow child self-regulation • Avoid conflict • May be very conscientious and engaged • Are lax in rules and monitoring of behavior
Low Nurturance	Authoritarian (High Control) • Set absolute standards • Stress obedience • Tend to model more aggressive responses to conflict or problems • Make high demands based on child's maturity	Uninvolved • Show little interest or attachment • Provide little or no direction • May be neglectful

So, What's the Problem?

Despite its ubiquitous nature and well-intended purposes, information about parenting suffers from at least three problems. As they think about what parents know and do, teachers need to consider carefully the quality of the information parents receive, how it is delivered, and finally the difficulty parents may have in applying it.

The *quality* of much of the information available to parents and about parents is good. But it is not *all* good, and even the good material has flaws. That is to be expected, because parenting is complicated by multiple and conflicting purposes, contexts, expectations, and demands. Some of the best, most thoughtful information fails to provide a level of specificity that some people may need or want. Like the best suggestions in the teen pregnancy information (e.g., creating communication-rich environments), many of the practices parents are encouraged to follow are more difficult than they sound. On the flipside, we find suggestions that may be easy to do (e.g., asking about homework each day), but the influence of which depends on the underlying characteristics of the parent-child relationship already established through more complex actions and practices.

We also have evidence that there may be cultural bias present in the analysis of parenting styles. Harris (1998) suggests that the "just right" or authoritative style of parenting, with its use of reasoning to establish a balance between love and limits, is "exactly what end-of-the-twentieth-century middle-class Americans of European descent think that parents *ought* to be" (p. 47). Others have also described differences in how parenting styles correlate with key variables among subpopulations (Darling, 1999). The authoritative style and its correlation to academic performance are largely associated with European Americans. The control factor appears to be more influential for boys than for girls.

There is also the problem of *delivery*. Parents do not have equal access to helpful information. Even when information provided is of high quality, some parents may have limited experience, education, and skills that affect their openness and understanding of material. They may not seek information on their own and may not know to pick up pamphlets in the cafeteria. Mass mailings of materials about specific issues or problems may not reach the parents who could benefit and may irritate those who do not need it. Most teachers know that good feedback is positive, specific, and immediate. It is hard to deliver supportive and useful information that can meet those criteria. Then there is the problem of unsolicited advice. I opened a fortune cookie once that read, "Unsolicited advice is seldom welcomed." Though I must plead guilty to continuing to give unsolicited advice, I recognize the truth in that statement. I remember a loving, nurturing, limit-setting parent of two successful children who once said, "I just wish the schools would leave me alone for awhile." Too much advice—not needed and not welcomed.

Finally, individual parents must *apply* information in their own unique contexts. Even with full comprehension and access to the best information available, parents have their hands full in working with their own beloved and *individual* children. Much of the advice is—as expected—easier said than done. And then there are the experts who caution parents to avoid the other experts! Cassidy (1998) reminds parents that no expert knows a child better than the parents do and that parents need to trust their instincts. Jeffers (1999) encourages a balanced approach to parenting and says that good parents "do not live their lives following the advice of childcare books" (p. 149). Instead, they recognize that parenting is tricky business and work hard to muddle through it with their children.

> "I used to believe my father about everything but then I had children myself and now I see how much stuff you make up just to keep yourself from going crazy."
>
> —Brian Andreas (1993, p. 22)

Experts offer advice; but it may be confusing, conflicting, too complicated, or too simple. Most parents turn to people they know for advice. They often look to other parents, including their own, for information about what to do with their children. Sometimes, parents may ask their children's teachers for information or encouragement. When *asked,* I found the following information helpful to share with parents as I empathized with their struggles.

WHAT'S A PARENT TO DO?

I think parents need to do three things: Avoid the extremes, focus on target goals for parenting, and keep trying. Though I know that this advice falls in the "easier said than done" category, I firmly believe in its logic, respectfulness, practicality, honesty, and potential for success. Let's look first at how trying hard and avoiding extremes can help parents stay on target.

Avoid Extremes

This is good advice for a number of reasons. First, it is an important component for healthy actions and relationships. Therapists Friel and Friel (1999) tell us that extreme behaviors and reactions are dysfunctional, and thus the "opposite of dysfunctional is dysfunctional" (p. 11). Consider, for example, a family whose members almost never spend time together versus families who spend almost all their time together, excluding nearly every outside relationship and interest. That's a big example.

Parents need also to avoid extremes in the little challenges. Think about how a parent might react to his eight-year-old's rude and disrespectful response to a request. What would be "off the line" at opposite ends of possible parental behaviors? I think one end would be an immediate, excessively angry physically or verbally abusive comment. On the other end would be a total lack of awareness of the child's need for discipline, which might take the form of agreeing with the child, encouraging the behavior, or believing that the parent deserved the rude response. In the center, we might find a variety of behaviors. One response might be to allow the child to finish before calmly and patiently explaining the rules of the house, the importance of respectful behavior, and the fact that disrespect to anyone will not be tolerated. Another middle-of-the-road approach might be showing hurt and anger, firmly invoking the consequences that have been established—perhaps the child will be sent to his room. Other responses are possible.

Think now of the variables that will apply to this one situation. Where are they at the time? What time is it? How typical is this for the child? What kind of day has the child had? What kind of day has the parent had? Are there people watching the interaction? Is the child embarrassing himself? Are others embarrassed? Is this a new behavior? Is anybody hurt by the remarks? Does the parent have a headache? The answers to these and other questions will explain a variety of responses by the parent. The answers help us to understand that there are times when parents won't be consistent when they should and times when they maybe *shouldn't* be consistent. Some responses will always be wrong, and some responses will always be better than others, *but* there are multiple, acceptable possibilities that, if not the best, are at least acceptable in the given circumstances. This is important for parents and everyone else to understand. There are more right ways than wrong ways; if we can stay in the middle, we're usually okay. Parents appreciate it when teachers understand this important idea.

Focus on the Target Goals of Parenting

I find it helpful to see the visual image formed by the concept of "staying in the middle." If we could take each concern, interaction, decision, worry, plan, and issue that parents face and place them like spokes around a wheel, it would soon look like the *prickly mess* shown in Figure 1.1, and parents know what that feels like. It's chaotic, confusing, sometimes good, and sometimes painful. We know that the extremes are bad and that somewhere in the middle is best. If we draw circles around the areas, we can begin to see just where the target goals are: right in the center. Parents—avoiding the extremes—should aim for the middle.

If a parent could be perfect, the center would be completely filled with correct decisions, appropriate and well-timed feedback, ideal limit setting, and model nurturing. No misses would escape that small area right in the center of the target. Wouldn't that be great? Yes, but impossible. Actual parenting looks different. There would be a larger center that accurately represents the limits of parents, children, and other people. The larger center also acknowledges a variety of legitimate response due to differences in style, culture, gender, and other variables. Some marks would be a bit off the center, but still on the target. And it might look different on different days—and different for different kids! There would be the admission and acceptance of imperfection.

Figure 1.1   Target Goals for Parents

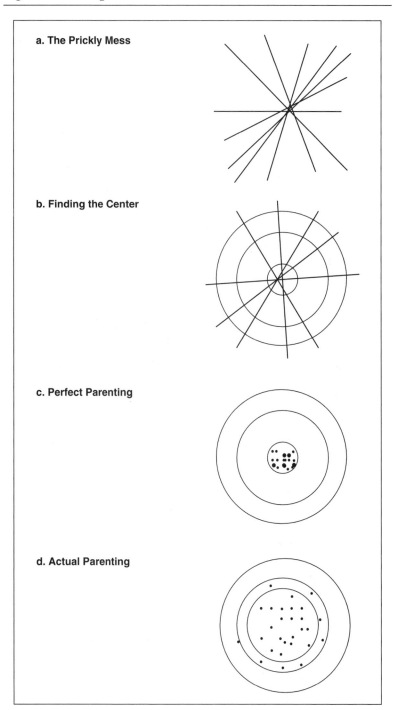

a. The Prickly Mess

b. Finding the Center

c. Perfect Parenting

d. Actual Parenting

Try Hard . . . and Keep Trying

Jeffers (1999) affirms what most parents know soon after a child is born: It's harder than we thought. And parents may wonder why no one told them. Perhaps they do hear it and think it will be different for them—or maybe it is just instinct.

Jeffers suggests that there is a conspiracy of silence. Parents don't want to tell how hard it is because they may, among other things, be fooling themselves, feeling ashamed, or feeling confused. "It is the very blessed parent who breezes through the parenting process without too many knuckle taps to the heart. If you are one of them, I suggest you kneel and kiss the ground and have compassion. Many aren't that lucky" (Jeffers, 1999, p. 103).

> What's a Parent to Do?
>
> - Avoid Extremes
> - Focus on the Target Goals
> - Try Hard and Keep Trying

Parents have to try hard, and they are not the only part of the equation. Coontz (1992) suggests that there is a myth of parental omnipotence. Parenting, she says, is both easier and harder than we may think. First, it is easier because it turns out that children are more resilient than we realize and can survive and sometimes benefit from our mistakes. It is harder because there are simply too many forces—out of parental control—that affect children's growth and development. For example, it is the "fit" between child and parenting style (just like between student and teaching style) that seems to explain success more than the style itself.

Other forces affecting parenting include class, background, income levels, conditions at work, and the pervasive presence and images of television. In addition, peer influence and pressure is a powerful force. Many people talk about the peer pressure that teenagers experience. Harris (1998) suggests that peers are the preferred models for children of *all* ages. She believes in group socialization theory and explains that it concerns learning how to behave in the presence of others. Children can determine what social categories they belong to at a young age. Early in life, they can categorize according to age and gender. They look for their peers and want to be like them. A child's goal is to be successful at being a child. Indeed, if children too carefully imitate the behavior of *adults,* they are likely to get into trouble.

We need to understand that there is not a simple, unidirectional, cause-and-effect link between a particular parent behavior and the reaction in the child. In fact, Coontz (1992) describes a long-term study in which researchers' predictions of which youths would be happiest and most successful as adults were wrong two thirds of the time—a worse result than if they had predicted at random. They had overestimated both the negative effects of family stress as well as the positive effects of a trouble-free childhood. Parental power and influence have limitations, but parents are still responsible for their children's health and safety. Some decisions and actions are better than others, and parents have to assume responsibility, meet demands, and make decisions *despite* the factors out of their control.

Parents are working to meet the target goals every time they think about or deal with their children. Rain or shine, day or night, big or little: They try to reach the target goals even when they have had a long day and are tired. Or when the kids have had a long day and are tired. They have to try hard to hit the middle, and they have to understand that they are not always going to be perfectly successful. Sometimes, it's a success just to be on the target.

Hewlett and West (1998) say, "Being a 'good-enough' parent requires providing a child with the gifts of love, attention, energy, and resources, generously and unstintingly over a long period time of time" (p. 30). Parents continuously and tirelessly aim for the target's center, and most of them somehow manage to hit consistently somewhere around the middle. And that, for the most part, is *good enough.*

THE KIDS HAVE A ROLE

Most parents can remember times when they did *everything* right and yet everything still seemed to go wrong! That happens because parents are not alone when it comes to parenting. The *children* are part of the equation, and they keep changing. Parents may have perfected exactly the right combination of food, timing, rules, and ambiance for a calm and successful dinnertime. But what happens when their beloved toddler simply changes his mind about his plastic dinosaur plate, the orange cup for milk, corn as his favorite food, and sitting next to his sister? Some children seem to change from day to day, and all children change as the months and years pass.

Children Grow and Change

Teachers and most others who work with children have studied child development. Most professionals understand stages of cognitive development and have an idea of what to expect from children at various ages and stages. When related to their fields of expertise, professionals also understand physical and moral development of children, adolescents, and even adults. Many theorists have analyzed the stages that humans go through as they mature. Countless textbooks have explored the subject and are available for extensive reading and study (see, for example, Santrock, 2004).

I think that Erikson's (1993) theory of human development, shown in Table 1.2, is a very useful way to understand how people change as they mature psychosocially and as they encounter new and different social interactions, expectations, and experiences. It is, of course, important to remember that theories of human development are culturally devised and thus should always be interpreted and applied carefully as one lens through which to view and understand behaviors (Trumbull, Rothstein-Fisch, Greenfield, & Quiroz, 2001).

Unlike professionals, parents may not have learned about the expected changes in their children throughout different stages of physical, cognitive, psychosocial, and moral development, but they know their own children and—consciously

Table 1.2   Stages of Child Development and Related Stages of Parenthood

Child's Stage in Erickson's Stages of Psychosocial Development	Age of Child	Parents' Stage in Galinsky's Stages of Parenthood
	Prenatal	**Image-Making Stage** Parenthood is an idea, a dream. Parents prepare.
Trust Versus Mistrust Babies find consistency, predictability, and reliability.	Birth to 1	**Nurturing Stage** Parents reconcile reality and image. Bonding occurs. Parental feelings of control/lack of control begin.
Autonomy Versus Shame and Doubt Children explore and make choices. They face dilemmas and learn what is acceptable.	1 to 3	
		Authority Stage This is the *peak* of control/lack of control. Communication is critical. Parents and children negotiate child's rights and power. Parents determine and accept scope of authority.
Initiative Versus Guilt Children make plans, set goals, and persist in reaching them. They respond to physical and social changes. There is frustration.	3 to 6	
Industry Versus Inferiority Children acquire and extend skills to wider culture; perform work; might fail; need to feel competent. They construct things and relationships.	6 to Puberty	**Interpretive Stage** *School* begins. Parents evaluate themselves. They interpret the world to children. They experience separateness, connection, and conflicting emotions.

(Continued)

Table 1.2 Continued

Child's Stage in Erickson's Stages of Psychosocial Development	Age of Child	Parents' Stage in Galinsky's Stages of Parenthood
Identity Versus Role Confusion Adolescents attempt to bring together experiences, identity, and place in society. They focus on self. They turn to peers.	**Puberty to Adulthood**	**Interdependent Stage** Another reconciliation between image and reality occurs, and parents shape new images. They experience less control and confront differences in power and control due to differences in ages.
Intimacy Versus Isolation Young adults are less self-absorbed. They can share with another, and the inability to do so is problematic. **They may become parents and enter the stages of parenting.**	**Young Adulthood**	**Departure Stage** Parents again adjust images of what actually happened. They take stock of whole experience. They build a new and separate relationship.
Generativity Versus Stagnation Adults work—producing things and ideas. They take care of others. They need encouragement from others.	**Middle Adulthood**	
Integrity Versus Despair Each person reviews and reevaluates life's worth. Acceptance of their imperfect life and their impending death leads to wisdom.	**Old Age**	

SOURCE: Erikson (1993) and Galinsky (1987).

or not—their own culture. They notice changes in the way their children look, behave, and approach tasks. They watch carefully the new things their children can say and do. They worry if their children are doing enough of the right things and at the right time. And they know how their children may compare to others in their family, neighborhood, or circle of friends. Parents may delight in the wonderful moments that occur as children grow and become capable of new and impressive feats, but they have an intuitive sense of the difficulties at different stages. As Jeffers (1999) says, no one ever mentions the "terrific twos, satisfying sixes, or great eights. . . . Just as we get over one terrible, turbulent, or tantrum stage, we seem to come face to face with the next" (p. 93).

We need to remember that kids are not passive. They do much more than simply respond or react. They think, decide, and act on their own. They are agents in their own lives. Their thoughts, words, and behaviors are not simply responses, but also causes. Kids are not only *done* unto; they *do* unto. They cause change in their parents and in others.

Parents Change and Develop Too

Galinsky (1987), in her extensive and influential study of parents of different backgrounds and ages, determined six stages through which parents move as they and their children grow up together. The most interesting theme that weaves through the stages is that of the clash between image and reality. Galinsky believes—and I agree with her—that as children progress through their stages of development, parents will be responding to their changes. At every change, parents must reconcile what *is* from what they *thought* would be. Parents do not always know that it is happening, yet this can explain a host of parent-child difficulties. What happens when athletic, trim, active parents are blessed with a child who is low energy, happier reading than playing, and chubby? What happens when a low-key parent bears a high-strung infant? What happens when parents comfortable with rigid rules and expectations meet their own child's rebellious nature? The clash between image and reality is real, and the bigger the discrepancy, the more difficult it is for families to face. Teachers benefit from this information when they think about the age of their students and the related stage of their students' parents.

Galinsky's six stages are shown in Table 1.2. As children mature, their needs change, and the tasks that parents must do will also change. The first three stages of parenthood occur before children enter school. First is the *image-making stage*, and it occurs before a baby is born. Preparation for parenthood is the activity of this stage, and the parents form images of what they and their baby will be like.

The *nurturing stage* lasts from birth to about 18 months or about the time parents begin to hear the familiar word "no." In this stage, the parents get to know their baby, his or her temperament and needs. They begin to wrestle with differences in personality and the real demands of parenthood—physical, emotional, and temporal. They form a strong bond with their baby. And, if they're honest, parents will describe the things they lose at becoming a parent: freedom, time, fun, sleep, privacy, and relationships (Jeffers, 1999).

The *authority stage* lasts from "starting to walk" to "starting school." The child is learning about his or her own authority, and the parents establish theirs. Parents of preschoolers can experience the range of human emotions directed at their child. The negative emotions—anger or resentment—will flash through most parents. The negatives can be surprising and unsettling, and some parents might feel shame. They are normal feelings and need to be managed.

The *interpretive stage* corresponds roughly to the elementary school years. Parents must let go of their children, and they have to reconcile their judgments of their children with the judgments of others. Teachers are of special concern to parents, because they have the power to influence the quality of the child's day. The child—out in the world—is seeing more, doing more, and subjected to more. Parents usually know by this stage that many others will affect their child's self-concept. One major activity for typical middle-class parents in this stage is to coordinate all of the others who are involved in the rearing of their child. They need to schedule appointments, organize church activities, and arrange for music lessons and sports leagues. Parents who are living in poverty are also involved in coordinating activities. For them, days can be filled with survival activities: getting to work with unreliable transportation, buying food each day because of money or food-storage issues, trying to manage child care, helping others who also struggle, and putting in "agency time" to get appropriate help from social services (DeVol, 2004). Most parents become experts on their child—and are appreciative when professionals recognize this.

The *interdependent stage*—adolescence—brings another period of reconciliation. Parents have to face a new person, one who is *almost* an adult. Many parents describe remarkable changes, not all of them good, in their children. Moms and dads also talk about their sadness at saying good-bye to the children they used to know. Once again, parents must work with their children to construct a new relationship with new forms of communication, changing roles, and adjustments to authority. There is a cruel irony for some parents because they often are cognizant of their personal aging process and feeling the changes: hair loss, weight gain, and sagging or bulging stomachs. And their children are reaching their peak. They are stronger, leaner, and better at many things than the parents. Most parents aren't jealous; they're happy for their children. Even so, it can be a complicated shift—and the demands of parental authority are still very much in place. Parents must continue to help their children safely negotiate their way into adulthood.

The last stage is the *departure stage,* in which the "children" are no longer children: They are adults venturing into the world as independent people. This departure is a process that in my experience can come in fits and starts. At this point, the parents are still adjusting their images of what actually happened. They take stock of the whole experience and reflect on what they think went well and what didn't. Galinsky (1987) found that parents at this stage who had the most positive sense of accomplishment were those who seemed to recognize early on that their children were quite separate beings. I remember when my husband, our oldest son, and I drove three separate vehicles to his new apartment. The vehicles were each packed so full with his belongings that visibility was a problem, and we knew that this was a big move, much different from the trip we had taken a year earlier to his first college dorm. We unloaded the truck, the minivan, and the compact car, and set things here and there in his apartment. The furniture went where he wanted it and the place was all his. We sat on the floor for a moment before we prepared to go, and our son held up a key. "Do you want to take this now?" he asked. It was the key to our house . . . *his* house. I told him that he could always keep a key to our house, but I have thought about that moment many, many times. It was a memorable symbol of his departure from one place to another, from one role to another, and from one relationship to another.

The stages are interesting to consider and useful in understanding the nature of this parenting task. Parents are of a certain age and will be in a particular stage of human development. They also will be in a particular parenting stage. They may have more than one child and the children may be at different stages. When we examine the theories and charts describing changes or levels of performance in children, their parents, or any of us, it is important to remember that the information is *general*. I find the information and descriptions very useful because they help me understand, recognize, and interpret the expected and unexpected behavior I see as I work with children or adults in *groups*. However, *individuals* rarely evidence all of the typicalities. Children are different. Parents are different. People are different. And those differences can lead to easier or harder lives, greater or lesser success, and a whole array of experiences. For parents, sometimes the differences lead to special struggles.

HELPING PARENTS WHO HAVE SPECIAL STRUGGLES

All parents have struggles, and a small percentage of parents have huge struggles that impact their lives, the lives of their children, and life in our society. Most parents are "good enough," but when they are not, they need our help. Teachers and other professionals who work with children are legally obligated to act when they encounter particular problems in families. Friends, family members, and even bystanders are encouraged to act as well. With knowledge, concern, and caution, we may be able to provide successful intervention to help end, manage, or prevent serious trouble.

Troubled Parents

Some parents are either off "the target" or barely on it. These troubled parents may be addicted, dysfunctional, or mentally ill (McEwan, 2005). They may have limited skills or resources. They may have cognitive disabilities. They may be experiencing a particularly difficult time in their lives that puts them and their children at higher risk for physical and emotional abuse. Parents who are barely on target can benefit from social services and similar agencies. Parents who are "off the target" may need to be controlled through the legal system.

Laws require reporting of suspected child abuse so that children will receive the protection they need. Those who know of problems must act, and doing so is difficult. We know that we may not understand everything. We may not be sure of what we see or hear. We often are afraid of making a mistake. Some of this caution is well placed. Hewlett and West (1998) describe a shift in how professionals who work with children and families have come to view parents over the past 30 years. A sizable minority have adopted a parent-bashing mentality, think that the American family is dysfunctional, and believe that a majority of parents have the potential to abuse children. This has led to a tremendous overreporting of child abuse. Of the 600,000 child abuses charges filed in the mid-1970s, 60% were substantiated. "Today, of the 3 million charges filed annually, only a third are ever substantiated and of these only a fifth involve elements of serious endangerment" (Hewlett & West, 1998, p. 115). Families have been torn apart by unfounded allegations.

Caution is needed, but so is proper action. Early action may prevent problems, and some experts encourage us to act *before* a horrible tragedy that too often is our impetus for action. Researchers advocate replacing "our typical pattern of after-the-fact notion of 'parent culpability' with a before-the-fact notion of 'shared responsibility'" (Coontz, 1997, p. 119). Providing children with safe, intact families is an important goal, and with the proper help, many parents can improve. In some states, child protective services have created successful programs that respond to reports of neglect or abuse in ways that both support families as well as ensure children's safety. Of course, in severe cases and for their health and safety, children may need to be moved to the care of other family members, foster care, or elsewhere. Coontz (1992) reports that children can make surprising progress in new environments.

What should we do to protect at-risk children and provide troubled parents the help they need? If child abuse or neglect is suspected, we need to report it. Though rules and reporting procedures vary from state to state, they generally require mandatory reporters to inform law enforcement agencies at once if a child is in immediate danger. If no immediate danger is present, but maltreatment is suspected, a different agency may be the proper contact, but the report still must be completed in a timely manner. Others, who are not mandated to report, are encouraged to follow the same procedures. The agencies that receive the report should be trained to protect the children, the rights of the parents, and anyone making the report in good faith (Minnesota Department of Human Services, 2003). Teachers, of course, are mandatory reporters, and school systems should support and train the teachers in recognizing and reporting suspected child neglect or abuse.

The following suggestions indicate typical procedures and guidelines when child neglect or endangerment is suspected:

- Gather information and keep clear records.
- Don't go it alone. Keep superiors informed. Work with mental health professionals, social workers, and/or law enforcement professionals.
- Know the legal rights and responsibilities of all involved.
- Keep focused on the child.

As we focus on the child, we can also remember that children can beat seemingly unbeatable odds, especially with support from others and through their own resilience. The keys to resilience—in addition to support from important person or persons believing in the kid—include feeling connected and successful in school, reading competently, having a sense of humor, showing initiative, and having intelligence, creativity, and spirituality (Rosenblum, 1999). We must remember that resilience is countered by risk factors, and the more risks that pile up, the harder it is for any child to survive. We must work to support the children and families who need it.

Parents With Troubled Kids

Some children have survived horrible experiences. In this section, however, we look at children who failed to live well under good conditions. These are children with particular temperaments or illnesses who have presented their parents with extraordinary trials, beginning as early as infancy. What may look like an out-of-control parent may be a parent who is working hard to keep an out-of-control child as reined in as possible. Our habits of mind (and mouth) tell us that the parents have done something wrong, but sometimes we are wrong to believe that. It sometimes really is the child.

I have had college students—soon to be teachers—come to me after class to say how much they appreciated my message about understanding and supporting the parents of their future students. They tell about how one of their siblings has been in serious trouble despite the efforts of their own loving parents. They add that sometimes their parents have fallen under public criticism and suffered greatly. Parents can indeed be crippled with shame when their children have committed public errors—often experimental drug use that gets out of hand or is caught (Meltz, 2000). I once asked a juvenile court judge if he thought that the parents of the teens he tried and sentenced were incompetent or uncaring. He said that though some did seem to have serious problems of their own, many parents clearly loved their children and had tried to help them with every resource available to them. Instead of unexamined censure, parents need support during difficult times so that they may provide the help and support their children need.

Sometimes, the difficulties lead to tragedy, even when the parents are doing everything they can do to help their children. Garbarino (1999) explains that boys commit 85% of youth homicides and, in about 90% of those cases, the boys have grown up with parents and general environments that are linked to such crimes. He describes their lives of abuse, neglect, and emotional deprivations, racism, poverty, and drug and gang cultures. In the aftermath of the 1999 school shootings at Columbine High School, however, he placed the two young killers among the 10% whose parents and lives did *not* fit the pattern of abuse. He wrote, "Most kids are like dandelions; they thrive if given half a chance. Some are more like orchids. They do fine while young enough be nurtured by loving parents, but wilt as adolescents subjected to peer competition, bullying, and rejection" (p. 51).

The temperamental, vulnerable children often make it through the elementary school years, but in the normal adolescent movement away from parents, they can't make it. The culture of adolescence today makes it hard for parents and professionals to distinguish between signs of the times and true trouble. Garbarino (1999) believes that we are

> too ready to blame good parents for how their children cope with a violent and coarse society. Even loving, attentive parents can lose children who are temperamentally vulnerable—if they develop a secret life, get caught up in the dark side of the culture and form dangerous peer alliances. And that's scary for any parent to acknowledge. (p. 51)

We must remember that even "normal" parents and "normal" children can run into a bump in the road, especially during adolescence. All children—even the "good" ones—lead what Garbarino and Bedard (2001) call "secret lives." As they move toward adulthood, they have to learn independence, and they learn it by *being* independent. Problems and struggles will arise. We can be thankful that most are solvable and temporary. We also can be thankful that understanding teachers who show empathy can make a difference. Box 1.1 shows how.

Box 1.1   Helping Parents Who Have Special
             Struggles

- Remember the demands of parenthood in general.
- Seek to understand specific troubles.
- Listen carefully and withhold judgment.
- Avoid blame and focus on positive action.
- Work with others to ensure the safety of children.
- Assist families in locating services and resources.

PARENTS LOVE THEIR KIDS

At the close of this chapter, I want to stress one important fact: Parents love their children. When we believe that, a world of opportunity awaits us. I think that, because parents love their kids so much, they may not be able to be at their *rational* best when their children are concerned. Parents are emotional about their children, and I think parents are supposed to be emotional. Psychologist Urie Bronfenbrenner tells us that a child develops through a process of complex interactions "between the child and somebody else—especially somebody who's crazy about that child" (qtd. in *Columbia World of Quotations*, 1996). For most children, that crazy someone is their parent. In Chapter 2, you will read about ideas for building collaborative relationships with these people who love their children so much.

ADDITIONAL RESOURCES

Books

Friel, J. C., & Friel, L. D. (1999). *The 7 worst things parents do.* Deerfield Beach, FL: Health Communications, Inc.

> The title sounds negative, but the book is not. It is one of my favorite books on parenting because it is accessible, reasonable, and supportive. The authors describe common mistakes that parents and families make, and then they suggest new and more helpful ways to approach the complex parental undertaking. They make good sense, and it is a fast read.

Galinsky, E. (1987). *The six stages of parenthood.* Reading, MA: Addison-Wesley.

> This book is not a fast read, but what I consider a "must read." Galinsky tells the parenting story sensitively and intelligently. Her anecdotes are interesting and her analysis is informative.

Harris, J. R. (1998). *The nurture assumption: Why children turn out the way they do.* New York: Free Press.

> A very strange and oddly entertaining book. When this book was first released, it created quite a hoopla. Many people were dismayed and angry at the author's assertions that it doesn't so much matter what parents do. She does say some things along those lines, but she says a lot more than that. It is an interesting and provocative book.

Jeffers, S. (1999). *I'm okay, you're a brat.* Los Angeles: Renaissance Books.

> I love this book. It is smart and funny. A student of mine who read it claimed, "It's not for the faint of heart." She found it a little disturbing to come face to face with negative feelings that parents may have from time to time. The book helps parents put many of the dimensions of parenting into perspective.

Web Sites

Aha! Process, Inc., available at www.ahaprocess.com.

Ruby Payne, a leading authority on poverty in America, founded the Aha! Process, Inc., publishing company. This site is their home page and is an excellent place to find resources and training opportunities.

Child Development Institute, available at www.childdevelopmentinfo.com.

This site was founded by Robert Myers, a clinical child psychologist. It is a very practical site, easy to navigate, and full of information about child development and parenting. There are many links to other useful sites.

2

Collaborating With Parents

*How Can Teachers Build
Relationships That Work?*

Scenario: "Is It Going to Matter?"

An inservice on inquiry learning was well attended by district teachers from all grade levels. The presenter, a classroom teacher from a neighboring district, was engaging and had included active participation throughout the morning. The teachers shared their own experiences and seemed interested in new approaches. In a question-and-answer session, one teacher raised his hand and made his statement: "This is all good, but until parents start providing a home life that encourages learning and supports us, is it going to matter?"

Teachers, like the one in the scenario, are influenced by prevailing attitudes and perspectives. We have heard and may have come to believe negative myths and stereotypes about families and how they have changed. Though educators recognize a link between parent involvement and student success, they tend to value only certain forms of support and fail to recognize other equally important elements (Fuller, 2003). Even student teachers often report that their cooperating teachers have attributed children's problems in school to the fact that their "parents just don't care" (Grossman, 1999). Research suggests, however, that parents *do* care and that "star teachers" see how much parents care, value this, and benefit from it (Haberman, as cited in Fuller, 2003, p. 281).

Like parents, teachers *also* are often misunderstood and underappreciated by groups they serve. Negative images and assumptions result in parent-teacher relationships filled with mistrust and defensiveness. Yet parents and teachers share common goals and complementary understandings that, when combined, form a powerful influence on student life and learning. In this chapter, you will read about the expectations parents and teachers hold for each other and a number of approaches that teachers can use to build the kind of relationships that make life better for teachers and parents—and for the children that matter so much to them all.

Before reading the chapter, you might want to take the self-exam found in Box 2.1. Your answers will provide food for thought as you move through the chapter.

Understanding Complementary Spheres of Knowledge and Influence

When working together, teachers and parents should remember that many of their *goals* are similar, but their areas of *expertise* are not. Their spheres of knowledge and influence are complementary, and together they hold an amazing amount of information about children. The teachers are knowledgeable about subject matter, pedagogy, and the general characteristics of the age group they teach. They also have a good idea of how each particular child behaves in the classroom, relates to other children or teens, and performs on class activities, assignments, and homework. They are experts at working with children in groups.

Box 2.1   Working With Parents Self-Exam

Think about your answers to these questions. Compare your answers to the themes found in the chapter.

1. What qualities do you think parents consider most important in their child's teacher?

2. What do you think parents do when they disagree with the teacher? Why?

3. What do you think parents do when their child dislikes the teacher?

4. What positive/negative experiences with their child's teachers are parents likely to remember?

5. What are some of the problems with parent-teacher meetings or conferences?

6. How can conferences help teachers, parents, and students?

7. What should teachers do in a successful conference?

8. What should teachers avoid in parent-teacher conferences?

9. In my mind, the ideal parent conference is one where the teacher can . . .

10. As a teacher in a conferencing situation, I think that I . . .

11. My planning for parent conferences is usually a matter of . . .

12. When it comes to my conferencing technique, the quality I most need to develop is . . .

Parents have a different sphere of knowledge, one that is equally important to the children and very useful to the teacher. Parents know their children's history, strengths and weaknesses, favorite foods, and whether they get scared at night or not. They have seen the children at their best and their worst, and they love them anyway. They can tell the teacher what is difficult about getting homework done and how the children feel about school. They also may have information about how the children learn that can help the teacher. And despite the fact that parents are often criticized for their lack of involvement in their children's education, most students report that their parents *do* know about the school and how well they are doing (Metropolitan Life, 2002).

Garbarino and Bedard (2001) remind us that some children have difficult temperaments and that to work with them requires two kinds of creative insight. We must be able to know a particular child as an individual . . . often the parents' insight. And we need to know about children in general . . . the insight of good professionals.

Here is a family story that is an example of what parents know about their children that can help teachers do a better job. My youngest son was a late talker. When he was about two and a half, he and I were standing in the kitchen, and his older brother and sister were at the kitchen table. He looked right at me and mumbled something that I couldn't understand. His 12-year-old brother looked up from his homework and said, "He wants a peanut butter sandwich." His five-year-old sister looked up from her coloring book and said, "Yeah. With jelly." I looked at down at my toddler, who smiled and nodded his head yes. He was a great listener and had a good sense of humor. He would laugh at the right times and at the right things even when he was little. But when it came to words, he didn't say that much.

I cried at the first kindergarten conference, because his teacher said he was in need of special help. She was brilliant as she helped me understand that the problem was developmental, that she knew he was smart, and that if I didn't want to sign the authorization form, I didn't have to. Of course,

I would do anything to get him the help he needed, but I also knew what it meant for children who had to struggle in school. (By the way, his teacher was right. By the end of first grade, he did not need additional special help.) I didn't know if every teacher would be able to see past his language delay to his quick wit and sweetness.

As time went on, my family realized that we did a lot of talking for him because he often took a little longer to think before speaking. We learned to give him a little time. When we asked him to do an errand or a job or his homework, we just took an extra few *seconds* to let him think about the task and ask questions before he began. We made sure he knew what we wanted, and then he could do *anything*.

I realized that if teachers could give him that same opportunity, his performance in school would improve. Teachers have many students, and perhaps they couldn't give him a few seconds for each assignment because the other students might need something too. But, as an experienced classroom teacher myself, I knew that not every student would need special attention at that particular point in a lesson and that "checking for understanding" would benefit other students as well. When I began to share this story with my son's teachers, most of them were willing to make that extra effort in order to reap great rewards (and we loved them for doing so).

Not all parents have the access to the information I have as an educator, but they have similar stories that can make a difference in the classroom. We know that most teachers ask for parent involvement. I hope that they all would value this parental knowledge and view it as one way parents support their children's learning.

What Do Teachers Mean When They Say They Want Support?

In a 2002 survey, more than 1,000 teachers were asked, "Which two of the following would most help your students be more successful at school?" (Metropolitan Life, 2002, p. 26). Sixty-five percent of the teachers chose "more parental involvement with child's education" as one of their two answers. The second most frequent response, given by only 32% of the teachers, was for students to receive "more one-on-one time with teachers." Teachers want parents to be more involved and more supportive of the schools. They first want parents to provide a safe and loving environment, and they worry about the children for whom that environment is apparently missing. Next, the teachers ask that parents spend more time with the children, ask about and supervise homework, and attend parent-teacher conferences and other school events. Teachers want more involvement, but many dislike what they perceive as parent activism, intervention, or intrusion (MacDonald, 1998).

Teachers realize that communication is the key. They strive to communicate frequently with parents, even though high numbers of students make it difficult. Most teachers inform parents when there are problems, but experienced teachers report more frequent positive communication with parents. They recognize the value in discussing their students' *good* academic performance, interests, and talents (Metropolitan Life, 2002). Teachers know that excellent parent-teacher communication will build positive relationships before problems occur (Whitaker & Fiore, 2001). The most successful teachers realize that good communication is a two-way (at least) proposition and that understanding what parents need and want is vital.

WHAT DO PARENTS WANT FROM TEACHERS?

Strickland (1998) tells us what parents do *not* want from a teacher: a lack of knowledge of subject matter, poor classroom control, unprofessional behavior, inability to diagnose learning problems, obsession about method, and improper goals. My colleague and I were interested in learning what the parents of our students *did* want from teachers, and we were fascinated by their reasonable and sometimes touching responses (Rudney & Fox, 1986). You will recognize some of the questions we asked because you thought about them when (and if!) you took the self-exam at the beginning of the chapter. How do your answers match what the parents said then and continue to say now (Rudney, 2002)?

What Qualities in a Teacher Are Most Important to Parents?

Parents have much to say in answer to the question of what is most important to them. They value subject-matter knowledge and the ability to communicate with them and with their children. As if they had read research on teacher effectiveness, they also list many teacher personality characteristics linked to student learning and classroom management (see, for example, Good & Brophy, 2002). The parents appreciate the teacher qualities of enthusiasm, patience, honesty, creativity, and firmness. Many liked to see a good sense of humor. These qualities establish a classroom environment that is both pleasant and focused on learning. They seem to be reasonable expectations.

The *top two* answers—listed by approximately 90% of the parents—are linked to the learning environment and beyond. The two things parents want first and foremost are that the teachers care about their children and know them as individuals. The desire for these qualities reveals how sensitive parents are to their children's emotional needs and how deep their concern is about their children's lives at school.

What Positive and Negative Experiences With Teachers Do Parents Remember?

Parents remember both patterns of behavior as well as isolated, highly emotional incidents. As shown in Box 2.2, their positive and negative memories revolve around similar themes. The difference is whether the desired action or attitude on the part of the teacher is present to a great degree or painfully absent. The parents remember fondly with heartwarming detail the times teachers showed personal interest in their children, gave them help when they struggled, and responded both to instructional and emotional needs. On the negative side, the parents struggle with what they perceive to be unfair or inconsistent discipline and poor communication. A few parents remember clearly the times when a teacher's unkind words brought their children to tears.

Box 2.2   Parents Remember When Their Children's Teachers . . .

- Show a personal interest in their children . . . and when they don't.
- Communicate openly and frequently . . . and when they don't.
- Respond to problems with concern and understanding . . . and when they don't.
- Give extra help and time to children when necessary . . . and when they don't.

What Do Parents Do When a Child Dislikes the Teacher?

Most parents report that their children like most of their teachers most of the time. If a child complains every now and then about the teacher, the parents say they try to empathize, discuss, and tell the child to make the best of it. Some parents say that they might have a conference with the teacher to try to ease the tension their child is experiencing. A very few say they would go to the principal if they remain dissatisfied. The parents' descriptions do not suggest a lack of support for the teachers. Instead, many of the strategies seem directed at helping the children cope with problems and building the child's sense of efficacy—that is, the child's belief, skill, and willingness to handle problems on his or her own.

What Do Parents Do When They Disagree With the Teacher?

In answer to the question of what they would do when they disagree with a teacher, most parents say that they would either contact the teacher about the issue or do nothing at all. A small number report that they would contact or meet with the principal. These seem reasonable responses, but I wonder about more typical behaviors that seem to be missing from their answers. I wonder if, when the parents say they would do "nothing," they mean that they would do nothing *at the school.* When prompted, parents do explain that they talk to other parents, just as teachers consult other teachers when there are issues or problems. There are drawbacks to this course of action for both parents and teachers, but there are also benefits. Clearly, it is not helpful for parents to broadcast even valid criticisms of teachers, and it is unethical for teachers to do so about parents. But *talking* to a trusted friend or colleague is one way to calm down, gain new perspective, and get a reality check.

Professionalism . . . in a Personal Way

Parents remember and value a teacher's professional *and* personal competence. They want the teachers to do their job— know the curriculum, communicate clearly, and manage the classroom fairly—but they want the teachers to be good people. They want the teacher to recognize their children are people too. The parents' hopes and expectations for teachers influence the way they judge and accept teacher actions and color the parent-teacher relationship. Parents and teachers hold high expectations for themselves and for each other. Some- times, the parents expect too much of the teacher. Sometimes, the teachers expect too much of the parents. Still, they can work together to achieve a common goal: helping the children learn and grow.

WORKING WITH PARENTS:
KEY STRATEGIES FOR TEACHERS

In the school setting, I believe that *teachers* have the professional responsibility to take the leadership role in establishing a true partnership. Box 2.3 lists the useful ideas that can maintain and improve high quality interactions.

Box 2.3   Key Strategies for Teachers

- Greet parents with respect and interest in their children.
- Solicit parent questions, comments, and advice.
- Think about homework.
- Develop "we-ness."
- Be prepared with interesting, meaningful information.
- Be honest . . . and patient.
- Be professional . . . in a personal way.

Greet Parents With Respect and Interest in Their Children

Teachers meet formally and informally with parents throughout the school year. They hold back-to-school nights, conferences, and spring open houses. They speak to parents on the telephone and communicate through e-mail and snail mail. They see parents at concerts and football games. They may also see them at the grocery store or at the movies. Though teachers should never hold impromptu conferences in public places (even if the parents should ask), they should always be respectful and kind. Equally as important, teachers must consistently show their interest in the parents' sons and daughters. Teachers must remember that the greatest "turnoff" for parents is when a teacher doesn't know the child (Ramsey, 2002).

This attitude of openness and hospitality is essential in formal, school-related encounters. Often, the first parent-teacher encounter is at a school-related function, and this interaction may set the tone for the relationship. We know that a first impression doesn't mean *everything*, but we also know that first impressions matter. Teachers, therefore, need to plan carefully for the *feeling tone* of their first meeting with parents. In addition to organizing materials and topics, they need also to plan on demonstrating their openness, interest, concern, and willingness to collaborate. Batey (1996) suggests teachers employ friendly smiles, welcoming posters, and respectful body language. They should think about and attend to individual and cultural differences (while being careful not to overgeneralize). They should be grateful when parents come to school and appreciative of other efforts that parents make.

At a school open house, a teacher once greeted my husband and me by smiling and saying, "Hi. It is only the good parents who come." We didn't know exactly how to respond! The comment really wasn't about us; it was about someone not there. I know it was intended as a compliment, but I don't think the greeting helped establish a welcoming atmosphere. If we hadn't been able to attend, would she think that we were bad parents? Would she talk about us to others? And what exactly was gained by her comment?

We also remember times when the greeting felt like one! One high school teacher saw our name tags and her face lit up. "I am so glad to meet you! I enjoy your daughter so much." The focus was on her student and our daughter, right where it should have been. Most teachers have learned this important part of working with parents. Respectful environments require consistency and generosity of spirit.

Solicit and Utilize Parent Questions, Advice, and Comments

We know that parents and teachers have overlapping spheres of knowledge and expertise. The professional skill of a teacher combined with personal knowledge of the parent will help children thrive. Teachers need to *ask* the parents for relevant information, accept it, and make use of it. Danielson (1996) has designed a thorough framework that outlines teacher responsibilities into four major domains, which are defined and further divided into components and elements. For each element, she has described what the teacher performance would look like at the *unsatisfactory, basic, proficient,* or *distinguished* levels.

In Domain 4, "Professional Responsibilities," Component C is called "Communicating With Families" and has three elements: (1) information about the instructional program, (2) information about individual students, and (3) engagement of families in the instructional program. The distinguished level of performance for the three elements can be characterized as meeting three criteria. First, information should be provided frequently, with a focus on both positive and negative aspects of student progress. Next, students are involved in preparing materials and contributing ideas for projects. Finally, parent concerns are handled sensitively. As much as I admire and use the framework with my own students as they learn to become teachers, I am struck by the absence of *soliciting parent ideas* in the framework. It still appears that the parents are being "done to," albeit sensitively.

After greeting parents, I often begin conferences by asking, "How is it going for your child at home?" This question always provides an interesting starting point and gives a context for the information that teachers are prepared to share. Often—because we know that children "loosen their belts" at home—parents will describe different frustrations with some of their child's behaviors or attitudes. At that point, teachers can sympathize and assure them that things at school were actually going much better (and I usually tell them that it is quite normal for the child to be grumpier at home!). Sometimes, there are problems at school *and* at home. With that knowledge, the parents and teachers can begin immediately to work together to solve the problems.

Occasionally, when parents say that things are going fine at home, the teacher actually is having particular problems with the student at school. Though it is possible that the parents are not comfortable in telling about a problem that does exist at home, in most cases there is no reason to doubt their assessment.

In any case, when the problem is at school, teachers should ask the parents for their suggestions on ways to help the child do better in the teacher's sphere of influence. Some of the adjustments I have made based on what parents have shared include adjusting due dates, changing seating arrangements, and selecting reading materials on different topics.

When asking for this kind of information, teachers should never pry or even appear to pry into personal business. Teachers should ask only what can directly affect classroom life. If they know they are not going to use any of the information, they should not ask for it. Of course, teachers will make professional decisions about what will or will not be done in the classroom, but parent ideas can be considered, adapted, and implemented in a variety of ways. If a parent does not want to share information, then the teacher should accept this and respectfully move on to sharing his or her own information. Teachers must always respect a parent's right to privacy, and any information shared about a child must remain confidential.

Teachers can solicit information in other ways too. One teacher I know asked the parents of her third graders simply to write a letter to her in which they could share anything they wanted her to know about their children. She said that some letters were long and some quite short, but from all of them she gleaned more information than she ever thought she would. Parents were anxious to write about their children. Another good idea is to have parents complete surveys (see Kyle, McIntyre, Miller, & Moore, 2002, for ideas). Surveys can ask parents about their children's interests and special needs, their own areas of expertise, and their scheduling preferences.

At the beginning of the year, teachers can ask parents what they hope their children will learn during the school year. The goal statements give the teachers a chance to discuss how goals are similar or different. Sometimes, the goals spark a good idea, and other times the teachers can explain why a particular goal (perhaps one that is too advanced for the grade level) will not be met that year. During the school year, a survey can ask parents how their children are feeling about school, what new behaviors or skills are present, or what concerns they might have. A survey at the end of the year could be part of a summative self-assessment that the teacher is making. Not all parents will respond to this or any one method, so teachers need to think of other ways as well.

Teachers must also be prepared to receive *unsolicited* information. If they truly want parent-teacher partnerships, then they need to understand that parents have information to share even when they are not asked to share it. Most parents are reasonable, and they have valid feelings and useful information. I encourage teachers to be open and accepting of parents as they share. This does not mean that teachers must immediately enact every suggestion, but it does mean that they must be willing to consider ideas and respond to them thoughtfully.

Two key words to remember from this strategy are *acceptance* and *action*. Both are required for meaningful collaboration. Both are required for shared decision making. Recognizing the value of parent input and demonstrating true interest in their comments will make a difference in a teacher's classroom success. Teachers can teach better when they ask, listen to, and thoughtfully use parent feedback.

Think About Homework

My oldest son wasn't always the most focused of homework completers. We used to laugh about how long it took him to decide he needed a pencil, find a pencil, decide to sharpen the pencil, find the pencil sharpener, actually sharpen the pencil, return to the table, and then remember what he was doing that made him need the pencil in the first place. Maybe some of you have watched that happen with your child or students too. Being a teacher myself, I wanted to support him in doing well and also to take responsibility for his work . . . the parent balancing act. So, I tried to be quiet when he took time to get organized and ready (but he would surely point out that I was not always quiet about it). Sometimes, we can laugh at problems with homework, but homework is serious business. It can have both positive and negative effects on families.

Homework has fallen in and out of favor throughout the 20th century. Cooper (2001) describes 30-year cycles, with the public demanding either more or less homework about every 15 years. In the 1980s and 1990s, more homework was encouraged as a defense against mediocrity and as a response to rigorous state-mandated standards. We are now in a backlash period, in which parents and others worry about children burned out at a young age and families unable to juggle so many competing time demands. Interestingly, it always appears to be the problem of an all-or-none approach. Homework, properly assigned with reasonable time and activity expectations, is a *good* idea. It can also be a battleground—between teachers and students, students and parents, and parents and teachers. Why? The answer is that it's complicated. It's a *good* idea that can go bad.

Research suggests that the completion of homework can be linked to higher grades and higher test scores (Cooper, 2001). That's good. The problem is that the benefits can vary according to subject matter, the types of assignment, the length and frequency of the assignments, the grade level of the students, the type of parent involvement present, and the needs of the particular child. Younger students and students with academic difficulties benefit from assignments on which they mostly are successful. A child benefits more from practice assignments on things that they mostly can *do,* rather than assignments for them to practice things they *cannot* do. Though that seems logical and obvious, it is not. Many teachers will assign extra work on the things that are causing students trouble so that they can learn them, but the students may need to learn these things *before* they are able to do the work. Students need their teachers to provide necessary instruction and guidance on their learning activities. Careful consideration of the impact of homework on families will help in building relationships with parents.

It is important for teachers to consider the economic, time, and skill resources that parents have available to them. We must be sensitive to the needs of families in a struggle for survival. Economic difficulties can create stress in families that teachers—so many of us with middle-class pasts and presents—have not experienced. Materials, space, information, and time all may be difficult to provide. To assist the children, teachers can adapt or cancel assignments, provide materials, provide extra instruction, and support or establish programs designed to help families with children in school.

Develop "We-ness"

We all have heard that children learn best when parents and teachers work together as a team. To create a team with parents, teachers really need to *believe* in this idea. Treating parents respectfully, asking for their opinions, and making use of the information they provide are crucial steps to building alliances—to developing "we-ness." When parents and teachers successfully become a "we," they can truly work as partners.

Partners appreciate each other. Teachers should recognize the variety of ways in which parents may support their children and the school. They should look for what *is* done for the families and not focus on what is *not* done. Teachers should thank parents for their efforts and recognize what a tough job it is to raise children (Ramsey, 2002). Of course, parents should do the same for teachers, but remember that the teachers need to take the leadership role.

Partners understand and support one another. Teachers should show their understanding by acknowledging, confirming, and elaborating on the statements parents make (Trumbull et al., 2001). Parents also show their understanding of teacher comments by acknowledging, confirming, or elaborating on them. If teachers listen carefully and don't hear those responses, they know that either the parents don't understand or have different concerns or priorities. In good communication, the priorities of all concerned are addressed and supported.

Partners—like teachers and parents—have complementary roles. Teachers can validate parents' roles by understanding—and letting them know they understand—that spheres of knowledge and expertise differ.

Be Prepared With
Interesting, Meaningful Information

Parents may indicate it in different ways, but most parents want to know four things from the teacher: how their children are doing, how their children's performance relates to how they "should" be doing, how the teacher will help, and how much the teacher appreciates their children. This may seem like a lot, but it is important for teachers to meet these needs.

Teachers usually can begin their interactions with parents by sharing their appreciation and enjoyment of the child. For some students, it is so easy! They are loveable and trouble free. For others, it is not so easy. I remember one year when I had one of those classes that all teachers have at some point during their careers. This particular class was filled with smart and unfortunately "smart-alecky" students. Group dynamics were strained. If I am honest about it, I just didn't find the students very likeable and felt bad about it. I believe that it is so important to establish positive relationships with each student, among the students, and with the whole class. That year it was a struggle. I knew I had to find something to *love* about those kids, and eventually I did. By talking to them individually, asking questions, and trying to get to know them, I eventually learned to love them. Jaime could repair bikes. Andrew loved to play *Scrabble*. Angelina was the most organized student I had ever known. A little appreciation on the teacher's part can make a big difference for the students . . . and that makes a huge difference for the parents. It is a win-win proposition.

Of course, the first three things parents want and need to know relate to teachers' professional obligations. To communicate student performance to parents, teachers need to be prepared to provide an appropriate and clear description of class activities and curricula, provide examples of student work and other measures of performance, and sensitively indicate how the performance does or does not meet standards. How this is organized depends on the grade level, subject matter, and style of the teacher. Some teachers have students keep portfolios, while others have a detailed student report using a computerized grade book. In every case, however, the summative information (grades and scores) should be supported with examples. Then, goals and strategies should be determined and discussed with the parents.

To be meaningful, all of this information must be communicated in language that the parents understand. Though teachers should not assume that the parents cannot understand what their children are doing, they should be careful not to clutter their explanations with professional jargon. Teachers need to avoid or carefully explain acronyms such as *IEP* (individual education plan) and shorthand language like *para* (for para-professionals). They might do the same for specialized concepts such as *time on task*, *formative assessment*, or *basic skills*. As professionals, teachers should know and use the language of their profession. But they need to know when to use it and when to check for understanding. Teachers can make things easier by explaining at the very beginning of the conference that the parents should interrupt at any time if the teacher is not being clear or if they should have something to ask or add.

Be Honest . . . and Patient

There are many "parent publics" that include working parents, single parents, teen parents, immigrant parents, gay parents, college-educated parents, and more (Ramsey, 2002, p. 60). Teachers communicate with all of these publics. Ramsey suggests that a teacher's credibility—beginning and ending with telling the truth—will increase the comfort of parents regardless of their background. Teachers must, of course, make judgments about what information and topics are relevant and appropriate to share with parents, but once that is determined—and as trite as it may sound—honesty really is the best policy.

When teachers honestly report to parents that everything is great, the only problem that might occur is that parents cry because they are happy. The problems arise when telling the truth means giving information that may cause pain for the parents. Even then, the truth is important, and parents deserve to hear it. However, they deserve to hear the truth delivered professionally, respectfully, and kindly. The feeling tone that teachers have developed and the rapport with parents that they have established will assist them in sharing the information. Those parents who already enjoy a positive relationship with the teacher are more inclined to trust the teacher's word even when the news is bad.

When I speak to groups of teachers about the importance of honesty, someone will typically bring up a time when parents took the child's side and did not believe the teacher. Most teachers (including me) have had similar experiences. Sometimes, the parents may be so hurt or shocked or embarrassed that they simply can't believe it—or don't want to believe it. Sometimes, a parent who is living in poverty may take the child's side as part of the actions necessary for survival (Pfarr, 2005). All parents will benefit from the teacher's empathy, calmness, and patience. For a few parents, teachers may need to consider the ideas presented in the section "Coping With Difficult Parents . . . or Parents With Difficulties," presented later in this chapter (see p. 52).

In most instances, teachers need to be patient. Their relationship with colleagues at the school requires it. Their work with large groups of young people requires it. Their collaboration with the parents of young people requires it. People make mistakes, have emotions, and have valid but conflicting perspectives. Teachers are people too, and they are some of the hardest working people I know. They, too, will make mistakes, be emotional, and have conflicting goals. They should not be afraid to admit ignorance or a mistake. By recognizing that they and others will be wrong now and then, they can avoid being defensive. They need to be patient with themselves as well as with others.

Be Professional . . . in a Personal Way

When I read essays in which teachers write about their professional development, I am most impressed when they show their professional knowledge with details that are unique to their own experience. The most reflective essays are those that reveal their professional actions in ways that show their own personal perspective, personality, and sensitivity. That is what I mean by being personal and professional. And this might remind you of what the parents said they desired in their children's teachers—all wrapped up in one phrase!

Teachers must develop appropriate personal relationships. Hospitality is personal. So are sympathy and empathy. Positive attitudes and cooperative spirit are also personal. Being a good person builds relationships, and those clearly relate to good teaching and successful learning.

Teachers must be professional. Whitaker and Fiore (2001) urge teachers never—and they mean *never*—to argue, yell, use sarcasm, or behave unprofessionally with a parent. Teachers must understand and abide by a code of ethics for the state in which they work; they should work collaboratively with other stakeholders; and they must understand and competently apply the knowledge and skills needed for their profession. As effective professionals, teachers influence others, and good teachers should offer "true professional help" (McGregor, 1960; though McGregor's work was conducted in the business setting, his findings are interesting when applied to schools). Teachers give true professional help by placing their knowledge and skill at the disposal of the children and the parents. When working with families, then, professionals are there to work and serve rather than make demands. Teachers should strive to be their personal and professional best.

Ask Not What the Parents Can Do for You but What You Can Do for the Parents

I love to suggest that teachers ask not what parents can do for them, but rather what they can do for parents, because I know that when teachers try it—even if it seems backwards to them—they are rarely disappointed. When teachers have worked hard to establish a positive, respectful, professional, and personal relationship with parents, they can safely offer help for the good of the students. I have met parents who have struggled with children who were troubled even as toddlers. After years of hearing about one problem after another, these parents are beaten. They have heard teachers criticize and share their own frustrations with the children. Some teachers may have told them what they should be doing at home to fix the problems. Whether or not they are parents in trouble or the parents of troubled children, these parents need teachers to understand and help.

I have watched tension drain from the faces of parents when teachers, instead of showing detachment or criticism, have said, "This must be hard for you. What could be done here at school that would help?" The parents may not know what would help, but they will appreciate a sincere offer. Moreover, there are things that teachers actually can do. They can use the information they have about child and parent development to provide information—when asked. They should be familiar with community resources and know how to access them.

Many sources encourage teachers to plan events and assignments that encourage parent involvement. Unfortunately, too often these activities represent the "what you can do for me" type of thinking. Well-meaning teachers sometimes plan such events and end up complaining about the parents who are not there or who did not do the assignment. Think about how the results might be different if the "what can I do for you" type of thinking were employed or if parents were *asked* what they wanted. Schools with strong and thriving parent education components will often ask the parents what they would like to study instead of offering a slate of predetermined parenting classes. One school experienced great success and fantastic attendance by offering computer classes for the parents.

Teachers cannot save every student, parent, or family in trouble. But when teachers draw on all of the services available and include parents in the problem solving, great things can be accomplished. When a teacher hears a suggestion from a parent, it is good to say, "If it is possible and will help, I will try."

COPING WITH DIFFICULT PARENTS . . . OR PARENTS WITH DIFFICULTIES

Some parents are a challenge. They might be angry and confrontational. They might be passive-aggressive. They might intimidate, anger, or confuse teachers. They may be difficult people, but we cannot always tell what the problem is at first. Ramsey (2002) provides a long list of pointers to help school leaders deal with angry parents. A common thread throughout many of the suggestions is that the professional needs to remain calm—in words, movement, and facial expression. When confronted by an angry parent, teachers and administrators can mask their own nervousness by lowering their voices, moving closer to the parent, and looking the parent straight in the eye (Whitaker & Fiore, 2001).

It is important for teachers to listen carefully to a parent who is angry or upset. I recommend that teachers start coping with a difficult parent with time, attention, and (sometimes) a pencil and paper. And I recommend that teachers remember that of all of the people in the room, it is the *parent* who has the most right to be emotional.

The first goal is to determine what the problem is. Angry parents need to be heard, so teachers can begin by taking time to listen and doing so without defensiveness. When confronted with an angry person, a teacher can say, "This is important and I'd like to write it down. It helps me remember and understand. Would that be all right with you?" Said without anger, this is a phrase that can calm some people, because they know that the teacher is taking them seriously. I personally have never had a parent refuse this request, but parents who are distrustful or wary of the purpose of record keeping may not want anything recorded. In that case, the teachers should simply listen, absorb the parents' feelings, and continue the conference.

When necessary and at good stopping points, the teacher can politely interrupt to clarify the problem or issue from his or her own perspective and to help the parent focus on the key issue. Encountering careful attention and respect, many parents will be able to adjust and move forward toward problem resolution. If not, teachers should stop the conference and reschedule. They can say, "I am sorry, but I don't think we're accomplishing what needs to be done. I would like to think about what you have said and to meet with you again soon. Let's look at our schedules. . . ."

By calmly and professionally responding to the initial confrontation or other sign of trouble, teachers can determine the nature of the problem and help work toward a solution. Box 2.4 offers a list of suggestions, organized by the likely source of the problem, that may be helpful when difficulties with parents arise. With professional reflection and analysis, teachers may discover that parent difficulties may be due to the situation, the parent, the student, or even the teacher.

Sometimes It's a Difficult Situation

A difficult person may actually be a person in a difficult situation. If it is a difficult *situation,* direct and open discussion will help. Families under stress can react in unusual ways. Sometimes, life events like illness, divorce, or change in employment can result in a temporary strain on the family. Other long-term problems, such as poverty or chronic illness, may cause unrelenting pressure. Teachers can give professional help by understanding the problem, assuring the parents that their child will receive the help needed in school, and, if necessary, making proper referrals.

Sometimes It's the Parent

There *are* difficult people, and some of them may be parents. Teachers who know that they must continue to work with a difficult parent can become discouraged. However, they can take heart in knowing that difficult people probably still love their children and that teachers can teach children

---

Box 2.4   What to Do When There Are Problems

If the problem is the situation,

- Focus on the needs of the student.
- Try open discussion first.
- Work to understand the problem.
- Be patient.
- Assure the parent that you will help the child.
- Determine if or how the school can provide or find resources.

If the problem is the parent,

- Focus on the needs of the student.
- Get help and support from administrators.
- Put some distance between you and the parent.
- Remain calm and professional.
- Focus on coping with the situation rather than "fixing" the parent.

If the problem is the student,

- Focus on the needs of the student.
- Begin or continue an open dialogue with the parent.
- Use shared knowledge—yours and the parent's— to problem solve.

If this time the problem is yours,

- Focus on the needs of the student.
- Consider alternate actions to try.
- Be willing to admit mistakes.
- Focus on future good will and success.

---

whether or not the parent is helpful. Teachers need first to believe in their own efficacy as a teacher.

When coping with a difficult person, it is useful to put some distance between the people involved, stop wishing the person were different, and formulate and implement a plan that breaks the interaction cycle (Bramson, 1981). When teachers distance themselves from the problem or person, they allow themselves the time to detach and reflect. During this time, teachers should avoid doing what all of us usually do when faced with a difficult person: We think about how good things would be if only the person . . . were different. In situations like this, that kind of thinking does us no good. Accept the person for who he or she is and make a plan.

A key part of a plan in dealing with a difficult person is changing the pattern of interaction. We are not trying to manipulate or trick the person by changing our own behaviors or reactions; instead, we are trying to establish a workable *coping* plan. Things that have worked (but not always) include changing the mode of communication, location, or participants. For example, if every face-to-face meeting results in shouting, the teacher could write notes, send e-mails, or make preemptive telephone calls. Instead of meetings in the classroom, the parent and teacher could meet in a conference room or other acceptable "neutral" territory.

I think it is very helpful to invite others to participate in meetings with difficult people. Another person can diffuse tension and may give the teacher a chance to understand the situation from different perspectives. It is important to remember not to spring another participant on an already disgruntled parent. I suggest informing the parent in advance and inviting the parent to bring his or her own advocate if desired. Notice that in this case, we are not trying to fix a difficult person, because we can't. Instead, we try to establish a plan that minimizes the trouble and maximizes the child's learning.

Sometimes It's the Student

I have always been interested to see how a student can sometimes manage to get teachers and parents in a complete uproar. They may conveniently leave out critical elements about their own involvement when explaining a school incident to their parents. They may cast blame on their parents when explaining a missing assignment to their teacher. Teachers should sensitively explore this possibility when getting to the root of a problem. Never assume. If teachers and parents draw upon their complementary spheres of knowledge, solutions may be found.

And Sometimes It's the Teacher

Sometimes, the teacher is a part of the problem. If the teacher is having serious difficulties, the administrator should know and should intervene. Often, however, a parent can have a problem that is the result of a competent teacher's unintentional error or a mistake in judgment. They may have hurt a student's feelings or acted in anger. They may have shown disrespect to the family. They may have difficulty seeing more than one way to accomplish a goal. I remember a high school teacher—a good one—who for some reason decided that a major assignment involving large displays constructed at home needed to be turned in on one—and only one—particular day. No one could argue with him about his right not to accept late projects (though there might be a good reason some times to do that with children), but the teacher would not even allow the students to turn them in early! One parent was beside herself with frustration. Previous plans were taking the family out of town on the day that the project was due and, though the project was ready to turn in on time, the teacher wouldn't accept it. The teacher said defensively, "Her son just has to arrange for someone else to turn it in for him." The parent did not find this a reasonable solution. What do you think?

Whitaker and Fiore (2001) warn us that if teachers feel defensive, it may be because they have actually played a part in a troubling situation. Be able to think about whether or not you as a teacher could have done something different. They say that offering an honest apology is one of the best ways to have the last word!

Conclusion

Parents love their children more than any other person does, and their concern and knowledge—when tapped—will make them powerful advocates. When untapped, their energy and love and concern can make them powerful adversaries. This adversarial relationship is avoidable. I hope that you have been thinking about your own perspectives on parents and families. Teachers, I hope that you have seen your own best practice reflected and affirmed in the suggestions made. I hope that you also have gained new ideas and suggestions for habits of mind that will strengthen your work and support future positive action.

We have focused on what individuals can do to work with, understand, and support parents. However, individuals do not work alone. Instead, we live and work in complex environments and as part of complex systems. Teachers and the families they serve find it easier to thrive when their school system, community, and greater society establish and support respectful communication. How we *all* can work together is the focus of Chapter 3.

Additional Resources

Books

Cooper, H. (2001). *The battle over homework: Common ground for administrators, teachers and parents* (2nd ed.).Thousand Oaks, CA: Corwin.

> This is a comprehensive and interesting book. Teachers will appreciate the synthesis of research that is presented in applicable ways.

Trumbull, E., Rothstein-Fisch, C., Greenfield, P. M., & Quiroz, B. (2001). *Bridging cultures between home and school: A guide for teachers.* Mahwah, NJ: Lawrence Erlbaum.

This excellent book focuses primarily on immigrant Latino families, but its description of the discontinuity between home and school has application in multiple contexts. The authors explain that their book focuses mostly on why parent involvement may be different from what teachers want or expect rather than on how to improve it. But in their explanations, they point to respectful and successful ideas.

Whitaker, T., & Fiore, D. J. (2001). *Dealing with difficult parents and with parents in difficult situations*. Larchmont, NY: Eye on Education.

Many of the stories and strategies in this book apply mostly to administrators. Still, it provides many interesting anecdotes and some occasionally non-common-sense methods of building positive, productive relationships with even the most difficult parents.

Web Sites

A to Z Teacher Stuff, available at www.atozteacherstuff.com.

This is the site for you if you like lots of ideas. Head to the "Teacher Tips" section, where you'll find information about working with parents and other things too. Many of the tips that I saw made good sense and fit in with the important ideas presented in this chapter.

Clearinghouse on Early Education and Parenting, available at www .ceep.crc.uiuc.edu.

Though the site focuses on early education, it has useful information about working with parents in general. For an excellent online publication, visit www.ceep.crc.uiuc.edu/pubs/connecting .html. Written by Mendoza, Katz, Robertson, and Rothenberg (2003), "Connecting With Parents in the Early Years" is a thoughtful, information-packed piece with excellent information about working with parents in many different life situations.

3

Advocating
for Parents

*What Are Powerful
Messages We Can Share?*

Scenario: "I Didn't Know How to Say It"

Rick was in his third year of teaching at a large school in an urban neighborhood. Most of his students lived in poverty. Some were homeless. When he first joined the faculty, he wanted to focus on teaching good lessons and doing all he could to help students learn. That still was his goal, but he had come to understand the immense struggle for his students and their families as they tried to make it through each day. He had to overcome some of his own fear and nervousness, but his mentors at the school had taught him to build relationships with families. And it had worked for him. Teaching was hard, but his students were learning every day. On a visit to his family home in the suburbs, he was disturbed by comments from a neighbor who seemed to dismiss his work, his students, and most especially his students' families. Rick said later, "I knew what I wanted to say, but I didn't know how to say it."

Throughout this book, we have explored assumptions, perspectives, and ideas in order to improve our understanding of parents and each other. We see that in our advocacy for children, we will often advocate for families. In this chapter, six messages of understanding and advocacy are presented along with the facts and figures that give them meaning and power. The six statements are reminders. They are big ideas written in simple terms (see Box 3.1). They provide powerful and positive concepts that we can share with others as we work together for the good of children. They might help people like Rick, on the previous page, know what to say and how to say it.

Box 3.1   Six Messages of Advocacy for Parents and Families

---

1. All of us have parents . . . and most of us become them.

2. Many powerful factors create misconceptions about parenting.

3. Most parents are good enough.

4. Successful families come in different shapes and sizes.

5. It really does take a village to raise a child.

6. Schools that advocate for families reap multiple rewards.

MESSAGE ONE: ALL OF US HAVE PARENTS . . . AND MOST OF US BECOME THEM

One of my students used the statement "All of us have parents, and most of us become them" as the opening line in an essay she wrote about how parents are portrayed and discussed in the media (N. Bevers, personal communication, November 10, 2000). For me, it is the first message of advocacy. The comment clearly states that when we talk about parents in general, we are not talking about somebody else—we are talking about ourselves. Approximately 90% of all adults become parents, and the active part of child rearing lasts about 25 years. According to Census 2000, more than one third of households in the United States included children under the age of 18 (U.S. Census Bureau, 2000). The children in these households may be our own—or they may be grandchildren, nieces and nephews, neighbors, friends, babysitters, or paper deliverers. In 10 or 15 years, they may be our doctors, lawyers, mechanics, and mayors. The connections to children, families, and parents reach all of us.

The Problem With Ethnocentrism: Like Me/Not Like Me Thinking

Most of us become parents, but we are not all the same. In parents, we see the full range of behaviors and attitudes, of successes and failures, of emotions and thoughts. We know that there are differences, and we can readily accept many of the differences. However, because we are human, we have a tendency to let *some* differences cause us trouble. The problem is that human beings often use *like me/not like me* as the unintentional measuring stick. Like me/not like me illustrates the concept of *ethnocentrism*, in which our own cultural norms and systems of belief are viewed as right and normal. The more someone is *like* us, the more we understand and the better we accept that person. The more someone is *not like* us, the more we will doubt him or her.

Harris (1998) describes the basic phenomena of group relations as the "preference for one's own group, hostility toward other groups, between-group contrast effects, and within-group assimilation and differentiation" (p. 136). Unfortunately, we often do not realize that we are doing it. We unconsciously categorize ourselves into many groups, and we unintentionally and sometimes unknowingly view those in *other* groups negatively. With an ethnocentric point of view, we view our own group as normal and often as best, safest, and most trustworthy.

This tendency has been studied in the workplace, where it was found that the further people moved from their own sphere of knowledge and experience, the less likely they were to trust in the ability, competency, and even good will of others (Barnard, as cited in Clark & Astuto, 1994). We can see another good example of this when we look at poll results reported by the Roper Center (2002). In a telephone interview, more than 1,000 adults were asked to grade public schools. Seventy percent of the participants who had children attending school gave their children's schools grades of A or B. Of the survey participants from the same community but without children in the schools, only 40% gave the schools in their community high grades. It would appear that their *distance* made it harder for them to trust in the school's adequacy and success. Workers, teachers, schools, *and* parents fall victim to like me/not like me thinking.

The Problem With Assumptions

Even when we have much in common with others, we still have a natural, egocentric tendency to value highly our own decisions, performance, and experiences while underestimating the value of others. We can look to management research for an interesting example of these concepts. McGregor (1960) suggests that a successful manager—like professionals in other fields—tries to predict and control human behavior. He adds that attempts to exercise this control are typically inadequate, and he cites juvenile delinquency, traffic fatality rates, and other social problems as evidence of our failure to control the behaviors of others.

> "Don't make assumptions. . . . By making this one agreement a habit, your whole life will be completely transformed."
>
> —*Dr. Don Miguel Ruiz*
> *(1997, p. 74)*

Our decisions are based on the assumptions we hold—whether our assumptions are accurate or not, adequate or not. McGregor (1960) mentions that when people don't do what we want them to—in other words, when we can't accurately predict or control their behavior—we lay blame not with ourselves but with them. An engineer, he says, does not blame water for flowing downhill, but managers blame people. McGregor went on to offer two contrasting theories of motivation based on assumptions. In Theory X, people, as egoists, assume that others will *not* do the right thing unless coerced and/or rewarded. Theory Y assumes that people accept and seek responsibility to reach objectives to which they are committed.

Of course, the same phenomenon happens when people make judgments about parents. In workshops and training sessions on working with parents, I often encourage teachers to think about how Theories X and Y might explain schools' relationships and decisions regarding parents. Teachers—and others—form opinions about parents based on a variety of images (Grossman, 1999). We remember our own parents and upbringing. We form attitudes about parents from professional experiences, literature, and colleagues. We see pervasive images from the media. We form opinions about others' parenting skills and even their character. The more similar they are to us, the more credit we give them for good things that happen and the more forgiveness and understanding we give when bad things happen. It is a natural human response, but it is not the perspective that leads to the most success.

If we follow Theory X, we assume that parents—especially those who are different in some way—will not naturally do what their children need. We assume that they need to be coerced into paying attention to their children. We give them activities to do with their children so that will spend some time together. If instead we follow Theory Y, we assume that parents naturally want good things for their children and will seek on their own to do what is necessary to help their children learn. Theory Y suggests that we communicate with parents in ways that respect their own interest and desire to tend to the needs of their families.

A Gentle Reminder

All of us have parents and most of us become them. When confronted with a broad generalization, this statement serves as a gentle reminder that parents are not a single group. If there is a problem, we need to analyze it and look for specific solutions. We can remind others that though it is not unusual to view those who are different or distant from us with a bit of suspicion, it is not the most useful or accurate perspective. By making a positive assumption, we can encourage better relationships, accurate understandings, and successful communications. Maybe, as suggested in the quotation box on page 62, our whole lives will be transformed.

MESSAGE TWO: MANY POWERFUL FACTORS CREATE MISCONCEPTIONS ABOUT PARENTING

"In recent years, big business, government, and the wider culture have waged an undeclared and silent war against parents. Adults raising children have been hurt by managerial greed, pounded by tax and housing policy, diminished by psychotherapy and invaded and degraded by the entertainment industry" (Hewlett & West, 1998, pp. 29–30). Could this strongly worded assertion be true? I believe it is. Watch the news. Listen to people talk. If there is a problem, people will often say, "If the parents had only. . . ." Look again at the target goals for parents in Chapter 1: Society too often views parents as though they were barely meeting target goals or completely missing them. As family advocates, we can let others know that if it were as easy as the parents "only" doing something, there would be few problems with children.

This second statement of advocacy opens the door to further conversation about assumptions. Policy decisions, media messages, and professional stances are affected by assumptions about parents. The pervasive messages that we hear affect our images and contribute to our assumptions. The result is often a set of strongly held misconceptions. Knowing this, we can look at things differently and make positive changes.

Remembering the Past

One of the most troublesome assumptions held by the public today is that parents these days are getting worse.

Many people believe that parents are not meeting their responsibilities the way they used to. This belief is strongest for single parents, working parents (especially working mothers), parents whose families are living in poverty, and others who are in some way different from "the norm."

In an explanation of the social purpose of schooling, Spring (2002) discusses the public's frequent claim that family and religion are collapsing. He describes the work of American sociologist Edward Ross, who declared that in modern society the school was replacing the family and the church as the most important institution for instilling values. Do you agree with Ross that families and churches today aren't doing their job? That they aren't doing the job they did 20 years ago or maybe 50 years ago? I may have tricked you a little with that question. Ross wrote those words in the 1890s! In reality, there is evidence that things aren't getting worse, and some things may be getting better.

Consider the following historical information. Harris (1998) suggests that the close affection parents feel for their offspring is a fairly recent occurrence in western society. In other eras and in many places, childhood was a very difficult and dangerous time. Children were considered possessions of their parents and the parents were able to abandon and mistreat them without reprisal. The late Middle Ages may have been the worst time. Children were left unattended and neglected and had lower chances of survival. As technology changed the organization of work, men began to work away from the home. The home became less like a business and more like what we consider "homelike" today. General health improved, and families began to need less free labor from their children.

Coontz (1992) reports that, in colonial families, high mortality rates meant that marriages lasted less than 12 years. Many children lost parents at a young age, there was strict patriarchal authority, and children were exposed to sexuality. In the Victorian family, women were defined by domesticity, men were defined as breadwinners, and there was rampant child labor. In the Great Depression, extended family households increased, and poverty exhausted people not only financially but emotionally and physically as well.

The notion of the typicality of the traditional family has rested on the backs of the working poor—often women of color. In the Victorian family in the United States, the sexual division of labor "depended on the existence of African-American, immigrant, and working-class families with very different age and gender roles. Sentimentalization of middle-class family life justified terrible exploitation of those other families" (Coontz, 1992, p. 65). The *Leave It to Beaver* families of the 1950s were not a return to traditional families, but rather a new invention and one that was a fluke. And interestingly, teen birth rates were higher then than at any time before or since. Women have always worked, but it is since industrialization that the home and workplace have been separated (Kamerman, 1980). Working women, now and throughout history, have helped their families survive and thrive.

Media Influences

Some of us remember a time when television would end for the night. After a late-night talk show and, on rare stations, a late-night movie, the station would actually sign off. Sometimes, there would be a test pattern, but the television shows were over. It was quiet. Those days are gone. Now, dozens of television stations are accessible 24 hours a day. If, by some chance, none of the 60 stations offers something you want to watch, in-home pay-per-view or a trip to the video store will allow immediate access to hundreds of movies. The programming is ever-present, and it contributes to a culture that has been called "toxic" (Garbarino & Bedard, 2001) and "poisonous" (Hewlett & West, 1998). What does this mean for parents?

We can first examine how the media affects how parents are perceived and, of course, the assumptions we make as a result. On the news, we hear about parents across the country who have harmed their children in horrible ways. Terrible things that a few parents have done are what make news.

Perhaps you remember a few years ago when a video camera caught a young mother striking her child who was strapped in a car seat in a parked vehicle. The video did not just make the evening news; it was played again on 24-hour news stations for many days. It was a pervasive image that contributed to our perception of parents.

Daytime talk shows also address parental problems. Who are the parents who will expose their problems on television? Why do they do it? How representative are they of most parents? I am not sure why some people would air their problems on television—whether they are parenting problems or some other personal struggle. I do know, however, that they are not representative of the general parenting public. Unfortunately, they add to our images and affect our assumptions.

Another type of message is the public service announcement. In most of these messages, we do not get parenting advice from a *parent*. Instead, we have a celebrity telling us to read to our children. We have a sports star reminding us to spend time with children. We have *children* telling us what good parents should do to keep them off drugs. The advice may be appropriate, but the delivery sends an additional message that may yet again negatively affect perceptions about parent capabilities.

In dramas and comedies, fictional parents also are contributing to our perception. They may be absent in shows where the children are raising themselves. More and more crime dramas show children as victims of parental abuse. Comedies feature inept, bungling parents. People are watching and are susceptible to incorporating the nonrepresentative—and sometimes unreal—images into their general perceptions.

As problematic as it is for the media to shape our image of parents in unrealistic ways, a bigger problem is the effect that the media has on raising children. The mass media influence the development of children and adolescents in ways that are still being studied (Zill, as cited in Garbarino & Bedard, 2001; Walsh, 2004). Children do not need to go to adults for information; they can instead turn on the television. They receive information from the television even when they didn't ask for it (Postman, 1994). Children are exposed to adult language, topics, and activities. They are exposed to violence, rudeness, and lies. It is a dangerous and powerful model.

David Walsh (2004), president and originator of MediaWise, explains that the entertainment industry is a business and is in business to make money. As viewers become desensitized to programming that used to shock them, the industry will add more shock value. Humor, sex, and violence have the most power to capture our attention, and when the three are combined, many of us are hooked. *Many of our children are hooked.* People in the industry and others say that it is the parents' responsibility to monitor their children's viewing habits. I mostly agree. We need, however, to recognize the difficulty of the task. Parents need to sleep and teenagers may still be awake. The family hour barely exists. The media target children and adolescents.

Habits of Mind

A principal giving an interesting presentation on how to interview well for a teaching job to a large group of preservice teachers closes with an appeal to the students to go into teaching with their eyes wide open. One of the problems, he says, is that they will take on many roles. They will spend more time with the students than the parents do. Several in the group nod in agreement.

This story is an example of a habit of mind that does not help us work well with families. It sends a negative message about parents—this time to a room full of future teachers—and it isn't true. Parents spend an average of more than 29 hours of engaged or available time a week with their children (Sandberg & Hofferth, 2001), and that number would be multiplied by 52 weeks. And they are sharing those hours with an average of one or two children—not a classroom of 20, 30, or more!

This is an example of the way image and assumption work together to create an opinion, a way of thinking, a habit of mind. As people listen to the pervasive messages and tuck them into their own ways of understanding the world, habits of mind develop. Box 3.2 reveals other misconceptions, as well as their more helpful counterparts. The great news is that we can change habits of mind, and we can respectfully inform others of facts and perspectives that can help them develop positive habits of mind as well.

Box 3.2   Helpful Habits of Mind

When you hear this:	*Try this:*
Parents these days just don't care.	Most parents care a lot. Some have real struggles.
If the parents would just. . . .	If only it were easy. It really is difficult for parents to. . . .
Most families today are dysfunctional.	Actually, most families are doing okay.
Working mothers aren't spending the time they need to with their children.	Most working mothers have had to figure out how to get their work done and spend time with their children. I wonder if the school could . . . .
These single parents just don't. . . .	Most single parents have their children as their top priority. I wonder if the school could . . . .
Those poor kids. There's no mom at home.	Many dads have to juggle career and family too. Luckily, most parents have good support systems. I wonder if the school could. . . .

The Real Deal

Today's parents do contend with multiple factors that make raising children difficult. Technology has opened the world to people of all ages. It is harder and harder to control the adult information that is accessible to children 24 hours a day. Increased pressures and expectations at work have resulted in a longer American work week, with more weeks at work than our Japanese and western European peers (Sandweiss, 2004). Telecommunications have actually extended work hours because of increased expectation that workers will be online and available (Levine, 2000).

According to the 2000 census, more than 13% of households with children had incomes below the poverty level. In families with children under the age of five, the percentage below poverty level jumped to 17% (U.S. Census, 2000). According to the National Center for Children in Poverty (2004), families need an income of two times the federal poverty level in order for the parents to provide their children with adequate food, housing, and health care. Nearly 40% of children in the United States live in families whose income falls below this level. Families living below or just above the poverty line encounter difficulties. They often find it hard to meet basic needs, receive adequate health care and safety, find adequate transportation, and provide extra learning opportunities (Fuller, 2003).

Despite the many situations, attitudes, and forces that make parenting so hard, most parents are working hard to do right by their children. This is information that we can share as we advocate for families.

MESSAGE THREE: MOST
PARENTS ARE GOOD ENOUGH

The public views most parents negatively (Galinsky, 2001). We can speculate that the phenomenon is based on the onslaught of negative messages that we hear. We also know that it could be rooted in the human characteristic of judging others by the like me/not like me measuring stick. Most parents, however, are doing okay and they care—and care a lot. They care more about their children than the rest of us do. For us, when thinking about someone else's child, we are thinking in principle. We are thinking in general. We are thinking from the outside.

For the parents, the child is *real*. If they overreact or underreact, it is because they know the stakes are higher. Their child's health and happiness matter most to them.

Children's Health and Happiness

According to a 2002 MetLife survey, nearly half of students surveyed worried somewhat or a great deal about being safe at *school*, but only 16% of students said that their families were not very or not at all happy. That is something to think about when we talk about schools as the only safe place for some students. It's true . . . for *some* students, but not all. Students also reported positive feelings about their home life, and more than 50% described their families as very or extremely happy. Another 35% said they were somewhat happy! Most parents hug their children and say, "I love you" every single day (Child Trends Databank, 2003).

> "People are generally more praiseworthy than we have been made out. That is a little secret of our age, perhaps of yours as well. Not all the people, all the time, but there is a tenderness, a loveliness that outlives our cruelty and stupidity."
>
> — *Roger Rosenblatt* *(2000, p. 88)*

Many health indicators also added to a positive picture (Child Trends DataBank, 2003). Most parents are making decisions about their own health and the health of their children that contribute positively to healthy living. Full immunization rates reached a new high of 81% in 2003. Eighty-eight percent of children used appropriate safety restraints when riding in cars. More than 96% of children were born to mothers who sought early prenatal care, and more than 88% of mothers did *not* smoke during pregnancy. Additional good health news for children is that, in 2003, fewer parents (23%) smoked at all than did in previous years. Because of its link to other family troubles, alcohol use is also an indicator of children's health and happiness. Data indicate that 96% of mothers and 86% of fathers do not drink heavily.

An estimated 896,000 children were determined to be victims of child abuse or neglect in 2002 (U.S. Department of Health and Human Services, 2002). Even one child is too many, but the number—as huge and unacceptable as it is—represents a drop from 13.4 children per 1,000 in 1990 to 12.3 per 1,000 in 2002. The statistic means that 987 children per thousand were *not* determined to be victims in 2002. Interestingly, this rate of abuse occurred during a time of increasingly stringent standards. The number of substantiated cases of sexual abuse against children also decreased significantly, from 150,000 in 1992 to 89,500 in 2000, a drop of 40%. Multiple factors contribute to the substantial decrease, and one of the factors is a *true* decline in the incidence of sexual abuse cases (Finkelhor & Jones, 2004).

Time and Attention

Time and attention given to children is another indicator of good parenting. One worry—a habit of mind—about parents in the first decade of the 21st century is that so many mothers work outside of the home. We already know two important things about this worry. First, in the past, the work of mothers inside the home was frequently related to the family's livelihood and survival—not just to taking care of the children. Second, even when some mothers were staying home to raise the children, *other* mothers were making it happen by working as housekeepers, dressmakers, and other service providers. Still, it is a troublesome habit of mind.

Almost 60% of children have both of their parents working, and most single parents must work. Like the principal described previously, we may believe that the parents aren't spending enough time with their children. We have evidence, however, that most parents are doing a good job even when the structure of their families and employment has made it difficult.

In the sixteen-year time span between 1981 and 1997, children's mean time spent with parents in *all* family types *increased* despite changes in number of single parents and working mothers (Sandberg & Hoffert, 2001). In 1997, working mothers spent an average of 26.5 hours a week with their children. This is only slightly more than the 26.1 hours that stay-at-home mothers did in 1981. In 1997, stay-at-home mothers spent 32.05 hours with their children, almost six more hours a week than did their 1981 counterparts. The "time spent" included engaged and accessible time, both of which are important. Galinsky (2001) writes of "hanging around time" and "focused" time as being equally important. Small moments like bedtime songs and other "traditions" can make a big difference to the children, and parents are working hard to provide such moments.

Whether or not parents work matters less to the children than does the context of their employment (Galinsky, 2001). What matters most is how well the parents connect to the children, what the parents value and model, and how the children are priorities in the parents' lives. And most children know that their parents are paying attention. For example, more than 80 percent of secondary students reported that their parents know how they're doing in school, 75% indicated that their parents know who most of their friends are, and more than 50% said their parents knew what was important to them (Metropolitan Life, 2002).

Encouraging Learning

Most parents are also taking adequate steps to encourage success in school. Four out of five children are entering kindergarten with good social skills, the specific skills linked to better school outcomes (Child Trends DataBank, 2003). A similar number come with necessary preliteracy skills. Most parents of children in all grade levels report their involvement in one or more school activities. The highest level of involvement is K–5 (96%), with decreases shown as the children get older (92% for Grades 6–8; 83% for Grades 9–12). General meetings, meetings with teachers, and school events were attended by more than half the parents at all grade levels. Volunteering and serving on a committee were reported by slightly less than half of the K–5 parents and about a quarter of the Grade 6–12 parents.

When There Are Problems

Statistics indicate where there are problems for families as well. First, there are negative factors that are increasing. Among school-aged children across the country, there are increased rates of obesity and decreased time spent in vigorous physical activity. For children who live in poverty, there are disproportionately high rates of some diseases, lower access to health care, and a greater likelihood that they will come to school with lower levels of preliteracy skills. More than half of high school seniors around the country have used marijuana or other illegal drugs—a number that is too high even though it represents a sizable decrease over the past 25 years.

There are also problems when we consider the minority of parents who are *not* performing the important tasks or behaviors that most parents do. They include, for example, those who do drink too much, who do smoke while pregnant, or who do neglect the needs of their children. They are a *minority*—and a small minority, at that. But we want the best for *every* child and for every family. As explained in Chapter 1, there are some parents who have mental or emotional difficulties that put their children at risk for neglect or abuse. Their condition may be permanent or it may be temporary. Some professionals, including teachers and doctors, are required by law to report child endangerment; all people, however, are encouraged to do so. The general procedures are outlined in Chapter 1, and most counties provide clear information about local guidelines. Teachers should follow the procedures specified by their school districts, counties, and states.

One important thing we, as advocates for families, can do is to help others put the idea of "bad" parents into perspective. When we see a parent struggling, we will help them more if we assume that they do care. It will help us understand their behavior better—even if we disagree with a decision they made. It will help us talk in nonthreatening ways about things that have worked for us. It will help the parents respond in nondefensive ways. It will allow us to be better listeners, and we might learn something too.

Box 3.3 provides interesting data about most parents. The advantages to teachers who advocate for parents of knowing this data may surprise you. Burns (2002) observes that students thrive in classrooms where teachers openly demonstrated a high regard for parents and caregivers. "This striking affective influence on children's capacity to learn suggests that the quality of the mother-teacher relationship and not the measure of the mother might be the significant correlating variable with a child's success in school" (Burns, 2002, p. 28). By improving relationships with parents and serving as their advocates, teachers may change the relationship with their students in ways that affect student comfort in the classroom, willingness to work, and thus academic achievement.

Box 3.3   *Most* parents raising children today . . .

- Make sure their children use seat belts and car seats.
- Show affection for their children and tell them "I love you" every day.
- Attend school meetings and events.
- Don't drink too much.
- Don't smoke at all.
- Make sure their children receive adequate health care.
- Know how their children are doing in school.
- Know who their children's friends are.
- Spend more time with their children each week now than parents did in the 1980s.
- Keep their children safe from abuse or neglect.
- Live in two-parent households.
- Read to their young children.

MESSAGE FOUR: SUCCESSFUL FAMILIES COME IN DIFFERENT SHAPES AND SIZES

We know that there is not *one* kind of family. We also need to remember that there is not one kind of *successful* family.

Understanding the differences in families and their potential for success is important as we advocate for parents. We know that people discuss changes in family structure and worry especially about single parents, working parents, and families under stress. Some may translate the family *conditions* into a belief that the mothers and/or fathers will parent poorly and perhaps not even care (Perrone, 2000). If the parents are economically less advantaged, from a different culture, or speak a different language, the distrust or concern is even stronger. (Do you remember the *like me/not like me* measuring stick?) As we look at the different shapes and sizes of families, it is most helpful to remember that many factors will contribute to the health of a family. Friel and Friel (1999) remind us that there are no perfect families, perfect parents, or perfect children.

Moms and Dads

The percentage of children living in two-parent families has been relatively stable at 68% since the late 1990s. Most of the children are living with biological parents (Child Trends DataBank, 2003). About 1.6 million children (about 2%) live with their biological but unmarried parents (El Nasser, 2001). Advantages to the two-parent family include higher average income and, typically, a greater internal support system. Theoretically, there is more time to spend with the children because there are more adults to take care of the business of the family: There is a friendlier parent-child ratio! Even in this idealized traditional family, parents can struggle. As most parents will admit, children can put stress on a marriage (Jeffers, 1999). Parents must address their own differences in parenting style and values. Even when parents are in complete agreement, they can be worn down by an active toddler or a confrontational teen.

Many two-parent families are also dual-career families. This requires additional scheduling and child care demands, but again the demands are often shared by two adults. Two-career couples who have successfully balanced family and work often will devise ways to ensure that they and their children are happy. Strategies that successful couples have used include sharing equally in the parenting tasks, clarifying their own parenting values, and utilizing the support provided to them by extended family or the workplace (Haddock, Zimmerman, Current, & Harvey, 2002). Working parents of different race, class, and gender all view more time as the top priority (Hewlett & West, 1998). Many seek flexible solutions to time issues that include, for example, compensatory time off instead of extra pay for overtime.

Much of the child-rearing responsibility and expectation still falls to the mother. Most of the conversations around mothers as parents continue to explore the effects of the working mother on their children. You have already read about the time that mothers spend with their children and that it has actually increased a bit. You have read that the children do not mind that their mothers (or fathers, for that matter) work, as long as they are not too stressed out and as long as the children know that they are the top priority (Galinsky, 2001).

The father's role is also vital and special. Hennon, Olsen, and Palm (2003) explain:

> Men bring diverse strengths and capabilities to fathering, and no one model or mode is argued as being the best. Fathers are important; and while attempts to encourage more quality involvement with children is beneficial for families, schools, communities, and society, attempts to create androgynous fathers or to feminize the role may not be appropriate. (p. 292)

In fact, fathers may be essential because of their differences from mothers. The differences include goals, values, and styles. Some characteristics attributed more to fathers include problem solving, sense of humor, playfulness, and risk taking (Johnson & Palm, as cited in Hennon et al., 2003). It is important to remember that, ultimately, we must take individual differences into consideration. Galinsky (2001) reports that fathers have felt ignored by educators, for example, who may expect the mothers to take care of the family business.

Some children live with parents who are gay. For the most part, gay families have to do the same things that other families do. The parents go to work and, when they come home, they supervise homework and chores. They take their children to soccer practice. Of course, these households must also cope with discrimination and response to their being "different." The child may be the only one who has two mothers coming to the parent-teacher meeting (Barovick, 2002). The children or adolescents may reject or embrace opportunities to speak out on behalf of their families. Powers and Ellis (1996) tell a wonderful story about how a young girl shares the news of her father's homosexuality. She wasn't embarrassed, but she was unsure of the response. Indeed, the responses varied from shock, disinterest, support, and curiosity. Gay parents must become skilled at managing a full range of response as they protect and care for their children.

Single Parents

Since 1990, the number of households headed by single mothers has increased 25% to more than 7.5 million households (Kantrowitz & Wingert, 2001). About 9% of households in 1999 were run by single moms, and there were about 2 million families headed by single fathers. More than 50% of children born in the 1990s will spend at least a part of their childhood in single parent homes. Single parents can provide much support for their families, but this depends on many variables. In particular, a network of support is needed as the many demands of parenting are met. The more connections single parents have with others, the more easily they manage their complex lives.

Noncustodial parents—usually fathers—also have a difficult time. The fathers can feel a lot of pain at losing time with their children (Zimmerman, 2003). It can be like a grief process. Divorced parents who work to put the needs of the children first can make the experience less painful.

Single parents today are looking for new ways to survive. Zaslow (2002) shares the stories of several families created when the single mothers met—through Web sites for single moms—and made arrangements to share homes and responsibilities and to provide child care support. Many of the arrangements begin with economic purposes, but the resulting emotional and logistical support is vital.

Stepparents

About 7% of all children live with a stepparent. About 8 million children (approximately 11%) live with at least one half sibling and 2.1 million (close to 3%) with at least one stepbrother or stepsister (El Nasser, 2001). These families are blended families. Among the findings supported by many researchers studying blended families are the following (Fuller & Marxen, 2003). First, younger children tend to make the best adjustment. Not surprisingly, adolescents—who seem to have more trouble in many areas—often feel resentful of the stepparent, especially if they are of the same sex. And, as expected, the attitude of *all* of the adults involved makes a difference in the children's adjustment.

Less expected is the following finding, and it is one I believe we need to remember: Most of the blended families report that they are happy. Blended families need to be flexible and ready to work at conflict resolution. Children who live in blended families may benefit from an extended kin network, a higher standard of living, and happy parents (Fuller & Marxen, 2003).

What the Children Want

Children want to be loved and to have stability. They want their parents to do well . . . and to make the children a top priority. They want to feel safe, secure, and loved. They also want to know that other people think that their family is okay. That doesn't seem too much to ask, and it brings us to our next area of advocacy.

MESSAGE FIVE: IT REALLY DOES TAKE A VILLAGE TO RAISE A CHILD

The African proverb "It takes a village to raise a child" captures multiple issues about growing up in society. It recognizes the inherent difficulty of child rearing. It suggests that it is a job too hard for one set of parents. It predates by *many* years the recent assets research for healthy youth and adolescents. This research describes the internal and external assets needed for healthy development and includes the importance of community and of nonrelated adults who care about individual youth (The Search Institute, 2003).

Most of us, when asked to describe individuals who helped us become who we are today, will give credit first to parents and then to some other people who took an interest in us even when they—unlike our parents—didn't *have* to! I have several. Dorothy Nelson was one of the first. She was a good friend of my parents and one of my first babysitters. She loved to read and bought me books on every gift-giving occasion. She asked questions about things that interested me and was always *very* interested in what I had to say. She also let me play her records over and over so I could dance around her living room.

Lea Agre was another important person. She was a family friend and my afterschool babysitter all the way through elementary school. She let me go on field trips with her Cub Scouts. She would treat her own kids and me to warm glazed donuts after school on some rainy days. She was proud of me, but she also disciplined me if I needed it.

Mrs. Vance entered my life later when I was in high school. I met her because her son was my boyfriend's best friend. My boyfriend and I would regularly go to see Mrs. Vance after going to a movie or even instead of going to a movie. It didn't matter whether or not her son was there, and I wonder sometimes now if it bugged him. Sometimes, when we would stop by, other teens would be there visiting Mrs. Vance. She was like honey to adolescent flies. What did she do for us? Well, she listened a lot, but mostly she laughed at our jokes. She was safe and interested, loving and supportive, encouraging and nonjudgmental. She, Lea, Dorothy, and others gave me confidence to face the world outside my family and know that I would be okay.

How many of you, as you read this, started wondering about where my parents were in all of this? Why did I need a babysitter? Didn't I feel safe with my own parents? Were there problems at home that made me have to turn to others? Here's the story. My parents were great. My mother was a working mom and I needed a babysitter. They made sure I had a good one, and my dad picked me up about 4:30 every afternoon. He drove me to my piano lessons on Wednesday mornings and made me a special lunch on that day. My mom took days off work most years so that she could do special sessions with my Girl Scout troop or help me with a birthday party. When I was upset about something, I waited for my meltdown until I was home. My babysitters didn't raise me—my parents did. But very special adults were part of the village that raised this child.

Teachers are a vital part of the village. They are also in a unique position to help others understand and apply this important message (see Box 3.4). Raising kids is hard. Most parents work hard to do the right thing. They love their kids so much, but it is too big a job to do completely alone. How can we support each other? Supporting parents in this incredible task requires *and* results in community, trust, gratitude, and friendship. Besides parents and teachers, who are the members of this important village? Who are the members of yours?

Box 3.4   It Takes a Village to Raise a Child: A Word
From the Teachers

- Parents need support, especially as families change.
- Everybody has something to offer.
- Nonparents should also help discipline.
- Government should provide financial support for child services.
- We need a societal commitment to valuing children.
- We need to consider all of the cultural pieces—the child as a *whole* person.

Members of the Village

The first nonparent "villagers" that most children meet are their extended family. Children make connections to their grandparents and form very special bonds with them. Parents appreciate and need support from their *own* parents as they learn how to parent. In today's society, with more and more families spread across the country, it is not always as easy for families to develop the deep connections to their immediate and extended families. Still, family members are important parts of the team that raises each child. Some family members, especially grandparents, are the ones most likely to step in when parents are having severe troubles.

Friends are also part of the village. Because parents so often have many things in common with their friends, they frequently turn to them for advice and support. Friends provide tremendous gifts to children when they form relationships with them. The positive affect they have on children—and, even more important, on adolescents—is unmistakable.

Coworkers may be the most complicated of all members of the village. Because so many parents work, parenting responsibilities that have an impact on their work affect colleagues. While many workplaces are considered to be family friendly, others are not. Working parents may actually face antagonism from coworkers. Policies designed to make the demands of balancing child care *and* work more manageable for parents include flex time, emergency family time, day care arrangements, and tax breaks. Some coworkers claim that it is unfair. Workers who are young, single, and childless make up a fast-growing segment of the workforce and appear to be the most offended by the special benefits aimed at parents (Lawlor, 2000).

Burkett (2000) believes that whenever families get tax cuts, somebody else make up the difference. She states that by providing parents with privileges and benefits, we are violating the principle of equal pay for equal work. This view looks only at immediate and individual notions of earned benefits. Many of us think that children deserve our support even if we personally don't benefit, but some experts explain that there are *delayed* benefits, even for nonparents. *Future* workers, raised mostly at their parents' expense, will pay taxes and provide services to all of the aging population, even the nonparents who did not contribute to raising them. In fact, in a *USA Weekend* poll, 3 out of 5 parents and nonparents agreed that parents get a better deal when it comes to leaving work on time, but most people *also* believed that nonparents come out ahead in terms of pay, promotions, and plum assignments (Lawlor, 2000).

Strangers are part of the village too. A friend of mine told the story of watching a young mother struggle with crying children in a restaurant and watching also two young servers roll their eyes and discuss how their children will never be allowed to act that way. My friend looked at the two strangers and shared a bit of important information: Sometimes nothing works. I don't know if the message got through, but I've always been impressed that she said it. Most parents can recall a time when strangers made judgments on children. Parents also will share how much support it can be when they receive a wink and an understanding smile instead of a grimace and a furrowed brow.

What the Village Can Do

When we work together, we can do great things. The Search Institute (2003) conducted a comprehensive study of children and adolescents that resulted in a framework to guide communities and schools to create healthy environments for young people. They found 40 assets—internal and external— that are linked to the success of children and teenagers. The external assets reveal that healthy youth depend on the quality of support, empowerment, boundaries, and use of time in their lives. Many of the assets require *others* to work for the benefit of children. They represent a way of looking at youth, valuing them, and acting on their behalf.

The asset research emphasizes the importance of caring adults outside of the family—not because their parents don't care, but because that is how humans grow and develop. Children and adolescents need to know that, in the world outside of their family, they can still build relationships, experience success, and be valued. Communities can provide activities, support, and a sense of caring. Schools do the same when they establish and enact rules that create a safe environment.

Because of the importance of *others* in the lives of children, the Search Institute conducted a follow-up study of American adults—both parents and nonparents—to investigate their beliefs and actions about what children need from adults (Scales, Benson, & Mannes, 2002). The results of the study revealed remarkable similarity in the *value* that children and adults gave to specific adult behaviors. Adults and youth believed that the most important things that adults should do to help the children and youth were to encourage school success, teach shared values, and instill respect for cultural differences. When it came to *acting* on the valued behaviors, both youth and adults believe that the adults fell short on the behaviors they valued. Still, more than half of the students and adults surveyed believe that most of the adults they know do all three of the valued behaviors. In general, the students gave lower ratings than the adults.

Youth who are experiencing difficulty in school need even more connection with adults. According to the MetLife survey (2002), the responses of D and F students suggest that they were less connected with adults. For example, about 43% of them reported that their parents did not know what was important to them compared to the average student response of 29%. Their apparent disconnect with teachers was *even greater.* Seventy percent stated that their teachers never spoke one-on-one with them about their interests and things that are important to them. It takes a whole village, and these children need even more of us on their side.

Hillary Rodham Clinton (1996) reminds us that we all benefit from raising children with care: "Just as it takes a village to raise a child, it takes children to raise up a village to become all it should be. The village we build with them in mind will be a better place for us all" (p. 318).

Message Six: Schools That Advocate for Families Reap Multiple Rewards

Parent involvement is a common topic of discussion by school personnel. We discuss it because we know that parental involvement is linked to student success. We worry about how to increase parent participation at the school level, and we lament the lack of involvement by the parents who don't attend our meetings and whose children often are not meeting our expectations. Parent participation can take many shapes, but the one that bothers teachers the most is lack of attendance at school conferences, meetings, and other events.

Why don't parents come to school? There may be financial and logistical problems. Are schedules too rigid? Is transportation a problem? Perhaps the parents distrust or dislike schools. How were they treated as a student? How have they been treated already by school personnel? How well do the teachers and administrators communicate? There may be a language barrier not only for non-English speakers, but also for non-*jargon* speakers. For those who don't understand the educational jargon, it may be confusing or intimidating. For those who do understand it, it may be irritating.

> "The way schools care about children is reflected in the ways schools care about children's families."
>
> —*Joyce Epstein (2002, p. 7)*

Role expectations also have an effect. Some parents may view their role differently than does the school, and their perceptions may point to different behaviors. The kids themselves can be a factor—especially adolescents. They don't always want parents to come to school, and we can't always blame the parents for being confused.

Despite the many reasons why parents might miss opportunities to consult with teachers, some schools and individual teachers enjoy high levels of parental involvement. They have succeeded in creating a space in which parents can take an active part. These teachers and other school personnel have advocated for parents and families. They have worked as allies to enrich student life.

Here are the ABCs of advocacy that will help individual teachers become family advocates and parent allies. Advocating for families will not only increase parent participation, it will improve the lives of children.

Attitude and Atmosphere

Individual teachers can create a welcoming atmosphere for parents in their own classrooms. As outlined in Chapter 2, their attitude makes the difference. They will greet parents, adjust their schedules, and solicit information. They will work hard to know the children and respect the parents' efforts. And they reap the benefits. School-level advocacy means that the same principles are applied in classrooms, hallways, administrator's offices, and even the district office. Individual teachers who understand this can be allies for parents as the parents try to understand the system and meet the needs of their children.

ABCs for Parent Involvement

Attitude and Atmosphere

Buildings and Bridges

Communication, Collaboration, and Competence

Attending to attitude and atmosphere is critical, especially when dealing with people for whom school does not evoke pleasant memories or feelings. At the school level, this may mean *strategizing* ways to create an open and civil atmosphere, ways to involve parents that work *for* parents. It may mean finding ways to celebrate the ways that parents *are* involved (Rasmussen, 1998).

Grossman (1999) explains that the amount of respect parents feel from school personnel is more important in the school-family relationship than how much time the parents spend at school. In order for school personnel to value the many ways that parents are involved, they need to understand many aspects of the families and community. People make behavioral decisions based on their cultural orientations. For example, parents with a collectivist orientation to the world (unlike the majority of teachers who are white and middle class) will view their role as raising children who work hard and show respect and obedience to authority (Trumbull, Rothstein-Fisch, Greenfield, & Quiroz, 2001). Trumbull and her coauthors suggest that educators look carefully at the behaviors they see and attempt to view those behaviors from multiple perspectives.

Buildings and Bridges

The actual physical characteristics of the *building* matter. Schools that value parents make not only an attitudinal commitment, but a physical one as well. As family advocates, we can encourage school personnel to create physical space for parents. Is the décor pleasing and does it include family-friendly messages? Are there places for them to sit when they visit? Is there a room or place where materials of interest to them are available? What provisions have been made for parents with young children? Is there an area where the children can safely play while parents attend conferences? The answer to these questions should be "yes." If it isn't, then the school has the first topic of meaningful communication for their next parent meeting. Creating a physical space for parents is a task to do together!

> "I came to parent conferences at the high school. All the teachers were sitting at small tables in the gym. It was like a cattle call. All of the parents were waiting in lines and having to race each other to a teacher who might be open. And then we had to discuss our son's grades with other parents standing a few feet away. I tried not to listen to the other parents' conversations, but it was so public."
>
> —*High School Parent*

Buildings must also be professional workplaces. The facilities and their use should allow all participants to do their important work in the best way possible. Teachers should have adequate space for instruction, preparation, and conferencing. Conferences should be held in spaces where students' progress and performance can be discussed privately, confidentially, and respectfully. The buildings should be safe.

To get the parents to the school—if that is our goal—we need bridges. We need to understand what might be holding the parents back and then we need to work together to determine how to help them. According to the National Parent-Teacher Association (PTA), roadblocks to parent involvement are lack of time, not feeling valued, feeling unwelcome, not knowing how to contribute, not understanding the school system, parents in need, lack of child care, language barriers, special needs, and lack of transportation (National PTA, 2000).

For each roadblock, the National PTA offers "detours." These detours—or bridges—include sensible and doable actions. Schools can offer child care. They can arrange for transportation to school events or conferences. They can provide interpreters. And maybe the teacher can take the bridge to the parent instead of expecting the parent to come to the school. As one excellent teacher told a panel of judges during an interview for Minnesota Teacher of the Year, "I always have 100% of parents involved in conferences. If they can't come to me, I go to them!" To get parent support, we need to support parents. We need to put out the welcome mat and mean it. Box 3.5 shows six recommended ways to involve parents.

Box 3.5   Effective Parent Involvement

In order to increase parent involvement and to enhance student learning, schools should provide the following:

1. Two-way, meaningful communication.
2. Information about parenting and supportive home environments.
3. Clear information about how to assist learning at home and at school.
4. Opportunities and encouragement to assist and volunteer in the school.
5. Involvement in school decision making.
6. Collaboration between school, families, and community.

SOURCE: Based on the standards for parent/family involvement by the National PTA (2000) and Epstein et al.'s (2002) parent involvement framework.

The time factor is one of the biggest problems faced by parents who try to meet the expectations of school involvement. We need to remember that parents *are* spending time with their children and that many of them are doing it despite the multiple and competing demands of modern life. Schools can consider ways to build *scheduling* bridges too. Schools can ask parents in advance about the dates and times that work best for them. They can schedule smaller sessions around meaningful topics so that there are fewer time conflicts. Schools can provide flexibility in meeting times, and they can consider alternatives to face-to-face meetings that can still encourage two-way, meaningful communication. Parent meetings should, if at all possible, be scheduled at a time convenient to parents rather than to the teachers.

Schools can also tackle some bigger questions. Families would benefit from—and a majority of parents support—a longer school day and school year (Hewlett & West, 1998). Levine (2000) suggests important topics to consider. If, as we're told, the current school schedule is based on past needs of families in an agrarian society, then what prevents us from adapting the schedule to meet the needs of current working families? What if schools were the center for services that parents currently have to patch together? Would parent involvement increase?

Communication, Collaboration, and Competence

We need to strengthen true communication. Schools work very hard to keep the parents informed. This results in many pages of information that are handed out during the first weeks of school. Parents who struggle with reading may balk at the lists of rules, regulations, and legal notices. Parents who know the system well may recognize the literature's true goal, which is often to meet legal guidelines.

True communication is not unidirectional; it goes from school to the home and from the home to the school. True communication respects the lives and the stories of the people involved. By understanding parents' stories, we will communicate more effectively. For instance, one principal described how parents start the school year with hope for a new beginning. For the parents of children who struggle, the year may also bring disappointment, fear, avoidance, and sometimes restoration. It is similar to the grieving process (Checkley, 2000). The parents have experienced the loss of a hope, of a dream. The children may experience the same loss. So might the teachers.

As part of communication, teachers and administrators should think, ask, and listen. Then they should be willing to act. That is how communication becomes collaboration. How can we collaborate with parents in meaningful ways? First of all, we have to ready ourselves for conflict. Mocker and Wilmot (as cited in Fox, 1998) describe conflict at the interpersonal level as the interaction of interdependent people who perceive incompatible goals and interference from one another in achieving these goals. Conflict of course can be healthy. Fox (1998) views conflict positively and reminds us that it is based on perception rather than on objective reality. Often, people are mistaken in their belief that having different goals will lead to interference with the achievement of our own goals.

How can understanding conflict help teachers and parents work together? Are parents and teachers interdependent people? When it comes to success for children in school, they usually are. Do they perceive incompatible goals? Sometimes they do, but perception is not reality. In fact, when I asked my students' parents to write down their goals for the school year so that we could discuss them at conference time, we had the same goals almost all of the time. Of course, the details about how to *meet* the goals can create new conflict, but a shared goal makes progress easier.

Authentic collaboration needs to involve parents in decision making about the issues, policies, and practices that involve their children and families. The National PTA (2000), in its six standards for parent involvement, stresses that *all* parents must be included—especially working parents, single parents, or parents from different cultures. This level of collaboration requires systematic planning and high levels of competence from all segments of the educational community.

To build competence, schools can provide teachers, administrators, support personnel, and school board members with training about how to work effectively with parents and families (National PTA, 2000). The education could focus on many of the *messages* presented in this chapter. Understanding the facts and myths about parents and their lives is crucial to building good relationships. In addition, educators could build their understanding of cultural differences and the characteristics of culturally relevant teaching. This important perspective would enhance relationships with children and their families and improve academic achievement.

We remember, of course, that students also play a role in their success at school, their parents' desire and willingness to be involved, and their teacher's attitude toward both student and parents. Epstein et al. (2002) remind us that students are the main actors in their education and development, but when parents, schools, and community work together, they will encourage and perhaps motivate the students to do well.

PARTING WORDS

Thank you so much for your interest in families and your hard work for children and their parents. I appreciate the efforts that educators make when working with families to improve the lives and learning of children. Thank you for letting me share my

> "If children live with acceptance and friendship, they learn to find love in the world."
>
> —Dorothy Nolte (1972)

ideas, beliefs, and strategies for building positive relationships with these people we know as parents. As we all move forward in our journey toward health, happiness, and understanding, I hope we can love the children . . . and their parents.

Many of us agree with Dorothy Law Nolte's (1972) message in her poem "Children Learn What They Live." She reminds us that how children are treated affects what they learn. Negative experiences breed negative behaviors and attitudes. Positive experiences result in a better world. I think that others—parents and probably all of us—can thrive, grow, and improve with the same ideals. Teachers can be the leaders in creating partnerships with parents based on acceptance, friendship, and advocacy. The children will reap the greatest benefits of all.

ADDITIONAL RESOURCES

Books

Kyle, D. W., McIntyre, E., Miller, K. B., & Moore, G. H. (2002). *Reaching out: A K–8 resource for connecting families and schools.* Thousand Oaks, CA: Corwin.

> This is a very practical resource. The activities and message encourage teachers and schools with specific ideas for positive action.

National PTA. (2000). *Building successful partnerships: A guide for developing parent and family involvement programs.* Bloomington, IN: National Educational Service.

> This important handbook is suitable for both educators and interested parents. There is a very clear summary of research on parent involvement, and the central theme of including and respecting all parents is excellent. The book contains practical guidelines and some useful surveys, evaluations, and planning forms.

Web Sites

MediaWise, available at www.mediafamily.org.

> MediaWise is an initiative of the National Institute on Media and the Family, founded by David Walsh. The Web site provides the most recent information on all things related to media and its effect on families. It is a powerful initiative that has the true capacity to help us work together to make change.

National PTA, available at www.pta.org.

> This really is a fantastic site for a fantastic organization. This is where to go if you are looking to boost your understanding, encourage advocacy, or inform others.

The Search Institute, available at www.search-institute.org/families.

> The Search Institute presents assets research. Recent studies reported on their Web site explore various issues related to families. The site is current, comprehensive, and relatively inclusive.

References

A to Z Teacher Stuff. (n.d.). Retrieved February 5, 2005, from www.atozteacherstuff.com.

Aha! Process, Inc. (n.d.). Retrieved February 5, 2005, from www.ahaprocess.com.

Andreas, B. (1993). *Mostly true.* Decorah, IA: StoryPeople.

Barovick, H. (2002, April 15). Rainbow Network. *Time,* F10.

Batey, C. S. (1996). *Parents are lifesavers: A handbook for parent involvement in schools.* Thousand Oaks, CA: Corwin.

Bramson, R. M. (1981). *Coping with difficult people.* New York: Ballantine.

Brazelton, T. B., & Sparrow, J. D. (2003). *Discipline the Brazelton way.* Cambridge, MA: Perseus.

Burkett, E. (2000). *The baby boon: How family-friendly America cheats the childless.* New York: Free Press.

Burns, C. (2002). "Good" mothers and children's success in school: Re-thinking the correlating variable. In P. Erixon (Series Ed.), I. Nilsson, M. Bloch, & K. Zeichner (Vol. Eds.), *Monographi för Lärautbildning och Forskning* [Monograph on Teacher Education and Research]—*Monografier: Monographs on Journal of Research in Teacher Education* (pp. 21–35). Umeå, Sweden: Umeå University.

Cassidy, A. (1998). *Parents who think too much: Why we do it, how to stop it.* New York: Dell.

Checkley, K. (2000, November). Parents are people, too: Leading with empathy and compassion. *Education Update, 42*(7), 5.

Child Development Institute. (n.d). Retrieved May 15, 2003, from www.childdevelopmentinfo.com.

Child Trends DataBank. (2003). Retrieved September 21, 2004, from www.childtrendsdatabank.org.

Clark, D. L., & Astuto, T. A. (1994). Redirecting reform: Challenges to popular assumptions about teachers and students. *Phi Delta Kappan, 75,* 512–520.

Clearinghouse on Early Education and Parenting. (n.d.). Retrieved February 5, 2005, from www.ceep.crc.uiuc.edu.

Clinton, H. R. (1996). *It takes a village and other lessons children teach us.* New York: Simon & Schuster.

The Columbia world of quotations. (2006). Retrieved March 9, 2005, from www.bartleby.com.

Coontz, S. (1992). *The way we never were: American families and the nostalgia trap.* New York: Basic Books.

Coontz, S. (1997). *The way we really are: Coming to terms with America's changing families.* New York: Basic Books.

Cooper, H. (2001). *The battle over homework: Common ground for administrators, teachers, and parents* (2nd ed.). Thousand Oaks, CA: Corwin.

Corwin, D. G. (1997). *Parent traps: Understanding and overcoming the pitfalls that all parents face.* New York: St. Martin's.

Danielson, C. (1996). *Enhancing professional practice: A framework for teaching.* Alexandria, VA: Association for Supervision and Curriculum Development.

Darling, N. (1999). Parenting style and its correlates. (ERIC Digest No. ED427896). Retrieved April 28, 2003, from www.ericfacility.net/ericdigests/ed427896.html.

DeVol, P. E. (2004). Using the hidden rules of class to create sustainable communities. *Aha! Process, Inc.* Retrieved February 5, 2005, from www.ahaprocess.com/files/DeVol_UsingtheHiddenRulesofClass.pdf.

El Nasser, H. (2001, April 12). More children live in traditional families, *USA Today,* p. 1A.

Epstein, J. L. (2002). School, family, and community partnerships: Caring for the children we share. In J. L. Epstein, M. G. Sanders, B. S. Simon, K. C. Salinas, N. R. Jansorn, & F. L. Van Voorhis (Eds.), *School, family, and community partnerships: Your handbook for action* (2nd ed., pp. 7–29). Thousand Oaks, CA: Corwin.

Epstein, J. L., Sanders, M. G., Simon, B. S., Salinas, K. C., Jansorn, N. R., & Van Voorhis, F. L. (Eds.). (2002). *School, family, and community partnerships: Your handbook for action* (2nd ed.). Thousand Oaks, CA: Corwin.

Erikson, E. (1993). *Childhood and society.* New York: Norton.

Finkelhor, D., & Jones, L. M. (2004, January). Explanations for the decline in child sexual abuse cases. *Juvenile Bulletin of the U.S. Department of Justice Office of Juvenile Justice and Delinquency Prevention.* Retrieved September 21, 2004, from www.ncjrs.org/pdffiles1/ojjdp/199298.pdf.

Fox, K. (Spring, 1998). Moving from conflict to healthy engagement in the classroom. *Faculty Development, 11*(3), 1–3, 11.

Friel, J. C., & Friel, L. D. (1999). *The 7 worst things parents do.* Deerfield Beach, FL: Health Communications, Inc.

Fuller, M. L. (2003). Poverty. In G. Olsen & M. L. Fuller (Eds.), *Home-school relations: Working successfully with parents and families* (2nd ed., pp. 273–289). Boston: Allyn & Bacon.

Fuller, M. L., & Marxen, C. (2003). Families and their functions—past and present. In G. Olsen & M. L. Fuller (Eds.), *Home-school relations: Working successfully with parents and families* (2nd ed., pp. 12–42). Boston: Allyn & Bacon.

Fuller, M. L., & Olsen, G. (2003). An introduction to families. In G. Olsen & M. L. Fuller (Eds.), *Home-school relations: Working successfully with parents and families* (2nd ed., pp. 1–11). Boston: Allyn & Bacon.

Galinsky, E. (1987). *The six stages of parenthood.* Reading, MA: Addison-Wesley.

Galinsky, E. (2001, April). What children want from parents. *Educational Leadership, 58*(7), 24–28.

Garbarino, J. (1999, December 20). Some kids are orchids. *Time,* 51.

Garbarino, J., & Bedard, C. (2001). *Parents under siege: Why you are the solution, not the problem, in your child's life.* New York: Free Press.

Good, T. L., & Brophy, J. E. (2002). *Looking in classrooms* (9th ed.). Boston: Allyn & Bacon.

Grossman, S. (1999). Examining the origins of our beliefs about parents. *Childhood Education, 76*(1), 24–27.

Haddock, S., Zimmerman, T. S., Current, L. S., & Harvey, A. (2002). The parenting practices of dual-earner couples who successfully balance family and work. *Journal of Feminist Family Therapy, 14,* 37–55. Retrieved September 30, 2004, from www.haworthpress inc.com.

Harris, J. R. (1998). *The nurture assumption: Why children turn out the way they do.* New York: Free Press.

Hennon, C. B., Olsen, G., & Palm, G. (2003). Fatherhood, society, and school. In G. Olsen & M. L. Fuller (Eds.), *Home-school relations: Working successfully with parents and families* (2nd ed., pp. 290–320). Boston: Allyn & Bacon.

Hewlett, S. A., & West, C. (1998). *The war against parents.* Boston: Houghton Mifflin.

Jeffers, S. (1999). *I'm okay, you're a brat.* Los Angeles: Renaissance Books.

Kamerman, S. B. (1980). *Parenting in an unresponsive society: Managing work and family life.* London: Macmillan.

Kantrowitz, B., & Wingert, P. (2001, May 28). Unmarried, with children. *Newsweek,* 46–55.

Kyle, D. W., McIntyre, E., Miller, K. B., & Moore, G. H. (2002). *Reaching out: A K–8 resource for connecting families and schools.* Thousand Oaks, CA: Corwin.

Lawlor, J. (2000, March 10). Parents vs. non-parents @ work. *USA Weekend,* 6–7.

Levine, S. B. (2000). *Father courage: What happens when men put family first.* New York: Harcourt Brace.

MacDonald, J. B. (2003). Teachers and parenting. In G. Olsen & M. L. Fuller (Eds.), *Home-school relations: Working successfully with parents and families* (2nd ed., pp. 92–110). Boston: Allyn & Bacon.

McEwan, E. K. (2005). *How to deal with parents who are angry, troubled, afraid or just plain crazy* (2nd ed.). Thousand Oaks, CA: Corwin.

McGregor, D. (1960). *The human side of enterprise.* New York: McGraw-Hill.

Meltz, B. F. (2000, May 21). Hiding parental shame only adds to the problem. *Minneapolis Star Tribune,* pp. E1, E6.

Mendoza, J., Katz, L. G., Robertson, A. S., & Rothenberg, D. (2003). Connecting with parents in the early years. *Clearinghouse on Early Education and Parenting.* Retrieved February 5, 2005, from www.ceep.crc.uiuc.edu/pubs/connecting.html.

Metropolitan Life. (2002). *The MetLife survey of the American teacher 2002—Student life: School, home and community.* Retrieved March 9, 2005, from www.metlife.com/Applications/Corporate/WPS/CDA/PageGenerator/0,1674,P2817,00.html.

Minnesota Department of Human Services, Children, and Family Services. (n.d.). Retrieved May 15, 2003, from www.dhs.state.mn.us/cfs/programs/ChildProtection.

Moore, S. G. (1992). The role of parents in the development of peer group competence. (ERIC Digest No. ED346992). Retrieved April 28, 2003, from www.ericfacility.net/ericdigests/ed346992.html.

National Campaign to Prevent Teen Pregnancy. (1998). *Ten tips for parents to help their children avoid teen pregnancy* [Pamphlet]. Washington, DC: Author.

National Center for Children in Poverty. (2004). *Rate of children in low-income families varies widely by state.* Retrieved September 28, 2004, from www.nccp.org.

National Institute on Media and the Family. (n.d.). Retrieved February 5, 2005, from www.mediafamily.org.

National PTA. (2000). *Building successful partnerships: A guide for developing parent and family involvement programs.* Bloomington, IN: National Educational Service.

National PTA. (n.d.). Retrieved February 5, 2005, from www.pta.org.

Nolte, D. L. (1972). Children learn what they live. *Empowerment Resources*. Retrieved March 9, 2005, from www.empowerment resources.com/info2/childrenlearn-long_version.html.

Perrone, V. (2000). *Lessons for new teachers*. Boston: McGraw-Hill.

Pfarr, J. (2005, January 28). *A framework for understanding poverty: Understanding our students*. Paper presented at the Winter Congress of the Minnesota Association of Colleges for Teacher Education, Minneapolis, MN.

Postman, N. (1994). *The disappearance of childhood*. New York: Vintage.

Powers, B., & Ellis, A. (1996). *A family and friend's guide to sexual orientation*. New York: Routledge.

Ramsey, R. D. (2002). *How to say the right thing every time: Communicating well with students, staff, parents, and the public*. Thousand Oaks, CA: Corwin.

Rasmussen, K. (1998). Making parent involvement meaningful. *Education Update, 40*(1), 1, 6.

Robertson, A. S. (1997). If an adolescent begins to fail in school, what can parents and teachers do? (ERIC Digest No. ED415001). Retrieved April 28, 2003, from www.ericfacility.net/ericdigests/ed415001.html.

Roper Center. (2002). *Education survey*. Roper Center at University of Connecticut Public Opinion Online. Retrieved March 19, 2003, from LexisNexis database.

Rosenblatt, R. (2000, January 1). A letter to the year 2100. *Time*, 82–88.

Rosenblum, G. (1999, September 19). Comeback kids. *Minneapolis Star Tribune*, E1–E2.

Ruiz, D. M. (1997). *The four agreements: A Toltec wisdom book*. San Rafael, CA: Amber-Allen.

Rudney, G. L. (2002, November). *Hearing parent voices: Strategies for advocacy and equity*. Paper presented at the annual meeting of the National Association for Multicultural Education, Washington, DC.

Rudney, G. L., & Fox, S. (1986, February). *Parents and teachers: Advocates not adversaries*. Paper presented at the annual conference for the California Association for the Gifted, Oakland, CA.

Sandberg, J. F., & Hofferth, S. L. (2001). Changes in children's time with parents, U.S. 1981–1997. *PSC Research Report No. 01–475*. Retrieved September 19, 2004, from the University of Michigan, Population Studies Center at the Institute for Social Research Web site: www.psc.isr.umich.edu/pubs/papers/rr01–475.pdf.

Sandweiss, L. A. (2004, April 9). The 40-hour work week—dead or alive? *IU Homepages*. Retrieved September 28, 2004, from www.homepages.indiana.edu.

Santrock, J. W. (2004). *Child development* (10th ed.). Boston: McGraw-Hill.

Scales, P. C., Benson, P. L., & Mannes, M. (2002). *Grading grown-ups 2002: How do American kids and adults relate? Key findings from a national study.* Retrieved March 9, 2005, from The Search Institute Web site: www.search-institute.org.

The Search Institute. (2003). Retrieved September 21, 2004 from www.search-institute.org.

Shore, P. A., Leach, P., Sears, W., Sears, M., & Weininger, O. (2002). *Your baby and child's growth and development: Your guide to joyful and confident parenting.* Toronto: Parent Kit Corporation.

Spring, J. (2002). *American education* (10th ed.). Boston: McGraw-Hill.

Strickland, G. (1998). *Bad teachers: The essential guide for concerned parents.* New York: Pocket Books.

Trumbull, E., Rothstein-Fisch, C., Greenfield, P. M., & Quiroz, B. (2001). *Bridging cultures between home and school: A guide for teachers.* Mahwah, NJ: Lawrence Erlbaum.

U.S. Census Bureau. (2000). Retrieved September 28, 2004, from www.census.gov/main/www/cen2000.html.

U.S. Department of Health and Human Services. (2004). *Summary child maltreatment 2002.* Retrieved September 21, 2004, from www.acf.dhhs.gov/programs/cb/publications/cm02/summary.htm.

Walsh, D. (2004, January 30). *Closing in on the "gap": The influence of media on student achievement.* Paper presented at the Winter Congress of the Minnesota Association of Colleges for Teacher Education, Minneapolis, MN.

Whitaker, T., & Fiore, D. J. (2001). *Dealing with difficult parents and with parents in difficult situations.* Larchmont, NY: Eye on Education.

Zaslow, J. (2002, April 15). Single moms unite. *Time,* F1–F3.

Zimmerman, K. W. (2003). Parents' perspectives on parenting. In G. Olsen & M. L. Fuller (Eds.), *Home-school relations: Working successfully with parents and families* (2nd ed., pp. 71–89). Boston: Allyn & Bacon.

Index

**CORWIN
PRESS**

The Corwin Press logo—a raven striding across an open book—represents the union of courage and learning. Corwin Press is committed to improving education for all learners by publishing books and other professional development resources for those serving the field of K–12 education. By providing practical, hands-on materials, Corwin Press continues to carry out the promise of its motto: **"Helping Educators Do Their Work Better."**